In this practical, easy-to-re[...] that holiness is in Christ, a[...] holy. This study of Colossians 3–4 leads us down a path of sanctification notable for both the grace of God and the grit of the daily battle that the Holy Spirit uses to lead us to strategies that produce victories.

**Joel R. Beeke**
President, Puritan Reformed Theological Seminary, Grand Rapids, Michigan & co-author of *A Radical, Comprehensive Call to Holiness*

The believer's pursuit of holiness starts with realizing that in Christ, he has already been made holy. In this collection of deep yet accessible sermons, Josh Moody helps the reader to avoid both legalism and passivity and to 'reclaim the real nature of gospel holiness.' *Everyday Holiness* offers soul nourishing help so that those who have received Christ will more faithfully walk in him.

**Erik Thoennes**
Professor and Chair of Theology, Talbot School of Theology, La Mirada, California
Pastor, Grace Evangelical Free Church of La Mirada

For far too many, holiness is a word that brings fear and dread. But for the Christian, holiness is the pursuit of joy. To be holy is to be more like Jesus. Everyday Holiness is a practical guide to holiness that is drenched in beautiful and rich theology. The best recommendation I can give this book is that I walked away from it wanting to be more like my Savior. Josh Moody has served the church well with this accessible and practical guide to a doctrine central to the Christian faith.

**Jenny Manley**
Author of *The Good Portion – Christ: The Doctrine of Christ for Every Woman*

This important exploration of the often neglected theme of holiness, based on Paul's letter to the Colossians, has a practical relevance which is urgently needed in contemporary Christianity. Writing out of his many years of pastoral ministry, Josh Moody's approach is accessible and uncluttered, thoroughly grounded in Scripture, full of godly wisdom and with many practical applications. His aim is to show us how to replace our cultural assumption, that life's task is to discover who we are, with a conscious, determined quest to become the person Christ designed you to be, which is the essence of holiness. Even a quick reading of this book will bring great benefits; but, much better, it deserves to be read carefully, pondered, chewed over, thought through and then its principles applied to all of life's circumstances. It is a book to be read and re-read many times. I warmly commend it, as a challenge to the will and a tonic for the soul.

**David Jackman**
Past President, the Proclamation Trust, London

…As we have come to expect from Moody's previous works, he serves as a wise guide not only to help us understand the meaning of the biblical message but to understand its significance for Christian living personally, in Christian community, in the home, in the workplace, and in the culture. Three insightful appendices further enable readers to understand what it means to be who you are in Christ, seeking to live a life of holy faithfulness and faithful holiness. I was both helped and blessed by reading this little volume and I know others will be as well.

**David S. Dockery**
President, International Alliance for Christian Education
Distinguished Professor of Theology, Southwestern Baptist
Theological Seminary, Louisville, Kentucky

EVERYDAY
# HOLINESS

*Becoming Who You
Were Made to Be*

# Josh Moody

CHRISTIAN
**FOCUS**

Copyright © Josh Moody 2022

paperback ISBN 978-1-5271-0725-0
ebook ISBN 978-1-5271-0906-3

10 9 8 7 6 5 4 3 2 1

Published in 2022
by
Christian Focus Publications, Ltd.
Geanies House, Fearn,
Ross-shire, IV20 1TW, Scotland.
www.christianfocus.com

Cover design by Daniel Van Straaten

Printed and bound by
Bell & Bain, Glasgow

# CONTENTS

*This one is for Elijah*

# Preface

This book focuses on one particular part of the Bible. I will inevitably leave out things that could (and some that should) be said about holiness by this approach. On the other hand, the issues being solved in Colossians are particularly relevant to our day. And by narrowing the focus we may be able to intensify the light and the heat, like a magnifying glass concentrating the rays of the sun.

The manuscript was skillfully edited by several people to whom I owe a debt of gratitude. Karen Meadows transcribed the recordings of the sermons, Carolyn Litfin gathered and arranged the material expertly and provided insight, Lindsay Olford collated the transcripts and suggested some quotations. I also want to thank Larry Dixon: this is now another of my books which has been the subject of his editorial work, and I am grateful for his diligence and skill. Thank you once again to Willie MacKenzie and his team. May your work continue to expand and flourish.

Josh Moody
Wheaton, IL, June 2021

'Holiness is nothing but the implanting, the writing and realization of the gospel in our own souls. There neither is nor ever was in the world nor ever shall be the least drop of holiness but what flowing from Jesus Christ is communicated by the Spirit according to the truth and promise of the gospel. Holiness is the shaping of our souls into the mold of the gospel, so that our minds and the gospel should reflect one another as face reflects face in water.'

John Owen[1]

---

1    I've slightly updated the language for the sake of a more pithy quotation for the frontispiece. For the full quotation, and the citation from Owen's works, see page 20 below.

# 1
# On Protestants and Prostitutes

It was not my finest moment. I grew up in England, just south of London. And as such, like many people at the time, my church background was the Church of England. I was no more than nine years old, I think. I was at school when someone asked me what kind of church I went to. I had heard a little bit about the history of the Church of England by that time and I knew that 'we were protestant.' However, when I tried to answer my fellow nine-year-old, instead of saying 'I'm a protestant,' I replied 'I'm a prostitute.' You can imagine the hilarity all around.

I think many of us have something of the same sort of confusion when it comes to 'holiness.' We probably know we should be—holy that is—but it feels like such a weird idea. And how do you spell it anyway? Is that 'wholly' or 'holey'? Does it require wearing horsehair shirts, or whipping yourself when you do something wrong? Is it a matter of cast-iron discipline?

Does it mean walling yourself up from the 'world' and protecting yourself from all nasty influences?

Those who grew up in 'fundamentalist' churches may still have scars from the odd ideas that some of those churches have foisted on us. I well remember one student coming up to me telling me about his hassles with holiness. I discovered that a lot of his fears seemed to stem from his very religious father who had told him not to have long hair because he needed to have a Christian haircut. The student was bemused when I (by then a pastor) had absolutely no idea what a Christian haircut even was. When he explained to me that it meant a short back and sides, I wondered aloud whether Jesus had a 'Christian haircut.' This seemed to help.

Sometimes we need to prick the bubble of prim misunderstandings about holiness for someone to even hear about the real Jesus. Another student came to Christ—or at least the journey began—mainly because I offered him a beer. He was dating someone at our church, and when I invited him back to our house one afternoon I asked him whether he wanted a beer. A year or so later I discovered that that was a turning point in his life. If this man who preached the Bible also could offer a beer as if it were the most natural thing in the world, then maybe he had the wrong idea about holiness after all. It sort of reminded me of Jesus—didn't He do something similar at a wedding?

Then of course there are the ethical issues that Christians (wrongly) have turned a blind eye towards. I still weep when I remember an African American who asked to see me as he was thinking of joining the church. We chatted for a while and once he seemed to feel comfortable he said, 'Can I ask you a question?' 'Of course,' I said. He told me how at a church in another part of the country a member of that church had called him by the 'N' word. He asked me what I would do if that happened. I said that if that happened here the person who did that would be put under church discipline, and if he didn't repent he'd be excommunicated. It's not all about lowering the standards and being more user-friendly. Some barriers have to be raised higher. Racism is out. In Christ there is neither Jew nor Gentile.

Tears are a good part of it. Oh, if only I could tell you a hundredth of what I've heard in pastoral counseling conversations. It would break your heart. The things people have done to each other. Sin is no joke. But then sometimes we take ourselves too seriously, and God not seriously enough. Laughter can be the best medicine. Isn't it harder for a rich man to get into heaven than for a camel to go through an eye of a needle? I still think that's funny. Have you seen a camel? Sometimes we should laugh at our foolishness—the foolishness of thinking that money is more important than our souls. Or thinking holiness is only for the professionals or super-spiritual elite.

Right at the core of a real understanding of holiness is this issue of being who you are. Holiness is not about becoming something or someone different. It's about being what Christ has designed you to be. Once you grasp that idea, and put it into practice, it will transform your life. And to that end, read on.

# 2

# *How to Begin*

*[1] If then you have been raised with Christ, seek the things that are above, where Christ is, seated at the right hand of God. [2] Set your minds on things that are above, not on things that are on earth. [3] For you have died, and your life is hidden with Christ in God. [4] When Christ who is your life appears, then you also will appear with him in glory.* (Col. 3:1-4).

'When I use a word,' Humpty Dumpty said in rather a scornful tone, 'it means just what I choose it to mean — neither more nor less.' 'The question is,' said Alice, 'whether you can make words mean so many different things.' 'The question is,' said Humpty Dumpty, 'which is to be master — that's all.' [1]

---

1    Lewis Carroll, *Through The Looking Glass*, (Macmillan, 1901), page 112.

That famous quotation from Lewis Carroll's *Through the Looking Glass* illustrates one common way to start: define your terms. How will we know what we are talking about if we do not denote precisely, especially if words today are made to 'mean so many different things.' Definitions are critical for clarity. That is particularly true with a subject like holiness because the word 'holiness' can conjure up emotions that are off-putting. It can feel legalistic. Burdensome. Unrealistic. And more.

A good definition of holiness can help us avoid the boil of legalism memorably lanced by the preacher Charles Swindoll:

> The problem with legalists is that not enough people have confronted them and told them to get lost. Those are strong words, but I don't mess with legalism anymore. I'm 72 years old; what have I got to lose? Seriously, I used to kowtow to legalists, but they're dangerous. They are grace-killers. They'll drive off every new Christian you bring to church. They are enemies of the faith. Other than that, I don't have any opinion![2]

Standard lexicons indicate that the word for holy in the Old Testament (שֶׁדֹק/ qodesh),[3] and somewhat similarly the word for holy in the New Testament (ἅγιος/ hagios),[4] imply that the idea

---

2    Charles Swindoll, interview with Howard Hendricks, *Veritas*, Vol. 7, No. 4, (October, 2007), page 6.

3    'Apartness, sacredness, holiness,' Gesenius, trans. Robinson, *A Hebrew and English Lexicon*, (Oxford, 1962), page 871; 'To be holy, spoken of a man who devotes himself to God, and thus separates himself from the rest of the people...to be sacred...set apart for God,' *The Analytical Hebrew and Chaldee Lexicon*, (Hendrickson, 2007), page 655.

4    Originally 'of the quality possessed by things and persons that could approach a divinity'; 'dedicated to God, holy, sacred'; 'pure, perfect, worthy of God'; 'consecrated to God.' Arndt and Gingrich, *A Greek-English Lexicon*, (University of Chicago Press, 1957), page 9.

of holiness is akin to 'separate,' 'other,' 'different,' or (as it is most commonly put) 'set apart.' Holiness is not about being boring or stuck in the past or overly rigid and legalistic. Holiness is being different, special, reflecting in some small way the otherness of God. The clock of holiness points to the Eternal.

But, important as that clarification is, the trouble with our view of holiness is not so much that we don't know what holiness *is* as that we don't know *how to go about attaining it.* Trying to attain holiness the wrong way has been a core challenge throughout the history of the world.[5] It was the problem of the Pharisees. It is the problem of many corrupt forms of Christianity (though at the other extreme, there may be perversions of religion that care not one whit for holiness). It was the 'fig leaf' covering of Adam and Eve,[6] and it was the essential nature of the problem facing the Colossian Christians too.

The Colossians needed to realize that as they, in Christ, already were 'holy,' therefore they were now to live in holy ways, setting their minds and hearts on following the pattern of Christlike living. So Paul tells them that Christ 'has now reconciled [you] in his body of flesh by his death, in order to present you holy and blameless and above reproach before him' (Col. 1:22); and therefore 'Put on, then, as God's chosen ones, holy and beloved, compassionate hearts, kindness, humility, meekness, patience ...' (Col. 3:12).

---

5    See Appendix 'A Brief History of Holiness.'

6    Genesis 3:7. Adam and Eve's attempt to cover their nakedness before God was inadequate in a similar way that wrongheaded approaches to cover up our moral nakedness with human generated so-called holiness are inadequate.

Listen to the renowned John Owen's definition. He defined holiness according to how we are to become holy:

> Holiness is nothing but the implanting, the writing and realization of the gospel in our own souls...There neither is nor ever was in the world nor ever shall be the least drop of holiness but what flowing from Jesus Christ is communicated by the Spirit according to the truth and promise of the gospel... [Holiness] is the delivery up of our souls into the mold of the doctrine of [the gospel], so as that our minds and the word should answer one another as face doth unto face in water.[7]

John Owen was, in the estimation of many, the greatest theologian that British Christianity has ever produced—though the Venerable Bede or Anselm of Canterbury might disagree with that assessment! At any rate, it is worth paying attention to what Owen has to say. First, holiness is empowered *by* the gospel. Second, holiness is becoming *like* the gospel—'as face reflects face in water.'

Paul is likewise calling the Colossians towards true holiness by showing them the right way to go about attaining it. He is urging them both to resist religious legalism *and* reclaim the real nature of gospel holiness.

## Resist Religious Legalism

Paul gives the Colossian Christians the spiritual antibodies to resist a particularly virulent form of religious legalism. This 'Colossian heresy' basically taught that if you followed specific religious rules and ceremonies, and had dramatic mystical experiences, you would become fully holy. The idea of 'fullness'

---

7   Owen, John, *Complete Works*, vol. 3, 'The Holy Spirit,' (Edinburgh, 1965), pages 370-371, 508.

seems to have been part of the rhetoric the false teachers used to entrap the Colossian Christians. Don't you want to obey fully? Don't you want the full experience? Paul counters this argument by pointing out the fullness Christians already have in Christ and so therefore we are to pursue only in Christ.[8] We do not know how the false teachers themselves would have described their message, but we do know Paul's devastating critique which is mainly found in chapter 2 of his letter to the Colossians.[9]

In Colossians 2:8, Paul says that the Colossian Christians must resist those who are trying to 'take you captive by philosophy and empty deceit'. The reference to 'philosophy' may indicate a Greco-Roman pagan philosophical influence, or just a cleverly deceptive yet vacuous theory. That the false teaching was 'according to human tradition' may mean commonly accepted but corrupt human ideas passed down to us, or a more specific form of that tradition in a religious form.[10] The false teaching was also 'according to the elemental spirits of the world'. What exactly these 'elemental spirits' were

---

8    Colossians 1:19, 25; 2:2, 9; 4:12.

9    If you want to follow the long-running technical debate about the Colossian heresy, you can read up on it in the various commentaries. For instance, F.F. Bruce *The Epistle to the Colossians, to Philemon, and to the Ephesians* (Eerdmans, 1984); John Calvin, *Galatians, Ephesians, Philippians, and Colossians* (Baker, 1974); J.B. Lightfoot, *Colossians & Philemon*, (Macmillan, 1886); R.C. Lucas, *The Message of Colossians and Philemon* (IVP, 1984); Peter T. O'Brien, *Colossians, Philemon* (Word Books, 1982); A.S. Peake, *Colossians* (Eerdmans, 1956); G.H. Thompson, *The Letters of Paul to the Ephesians, to the Colossians and to Philemon* (Cambridge University Press, 1967); Curtis Vaughan, *Colossians* (Zondervan, 1996); John Woodhouse, *Colossians & Philemon* (Christian Focus, 2011).

10   The two go together: human religious tradition tends to reflect in religious form the ideas that humans typically embrace anyway.

that Paul refers to is disputed, but they were probably part and parcel of the mystical emphasis of the false teaching. And, Paul says, the false teaching was 'not according to Christ'. *According* to tradition. *According* to mysticism. But *not according* to Christ.

Then in Colossians 2:16, Paul says that the Colossian Christians must resist being judged for not following the false teachers' religious rules and sacred days: 'let no one pass judgment on you in questions of food and drink, or with regard to a festival or a new moon or a Sabbath.' The Colossians were to resist being disqualified, or rejected, by the false teachers' exclusive religious club, if they did not ascribe to the false teachers' asceticism and mysticism, verse 18, 'Let no one disqualify you, insisting on ascetism and worship of angels.' Ascetism urges severe abstinence, for instance from necessary food or legitimate pleasures. The 'worship of angels' is another puzzle piece in the Colossian heresy, suggesting that the false teachers viewed angels as worthy of adoration like some kind of superhero demigod.[11] The consequence of all this false teaching, if not resisted, was a submissive bondage to legalism. Why, Paul asks in verse 20, 'do you submit to regulations—"Do not handle, Do not taste, Do not touch"...according to human precepts and teachings?'

---

11  It's interesting to compare how this text reads in different parts of the world today. For instance, the Africa Study Bible notes that, 'Some people live under the spiritual powers of this world. They are careful to avoid taboos and add extra special rules to Christian teaching, often from traditional African beliefs. Some believe the act of fasting will make them right in God's sight. Others try to understand angelic hierarchies and spiritual territories. But self-denial or special knowledge cannot change our sinful hearts or make us acceptable in God's sight' (*Africa Study Bible*, ed. John Susu, (Oasis International Limited, 2012), page 1751.

Finally, in Colossians 2:23 Paul summarizes the false teaching as having 'an appearance of wisdom in promoting self-made religion and asceticism and severity to the body, but they are of no value in stopping the indulgence of the flesh.' It was a human designed religion, a ritualistic, legalistic, mysticism—and what is more, *it was useless*, it was 'of no value'! Not only was this false teaching wrong, *because* it was wrong it was practically ineffective. It would not make you more holy. Therefore, Paul is saying, resist religious legalism.

## Reclaim the Real Nature of Gospel Holiness

But the Colossians must not only resist religious legalism, they must also reclaim the real nature of gospel holiness. To do that, they needed a much more exalted vision of who Jesus Christ is. As Paul famously put it in Colossians 1:15-20:

> He [that is Christ] is the image of the invisible God... by him all things were created... he is before all things, and in him all things hold together... in him all the fullness of God was pleased to dwell, and through him to reconcile to himself all things... making peace by the blood of his cross.

Paul is saying *this* is who Christ is. Christ is not merely a philosophy. He is not simply a set of good ideas. He is not only a teacher. He is not one among other spiritual heroes. He is far more than any of that. He is the image of the invisible God. He is before all things. In Him all the fullness of God Himself dwells. *This* is who Christ is. And therefore *because* this is who Christ is, Paul can persuasively exhort the Colossians to allow 'no one to delude you with plausible arguments,' with this false teaching about holiness (Col. 2:4).

What then is the right way to become more holy? The key principle is expressed in Colossians 2:6. Paul says, 'As you received Christ Jesus the Lord, so walk in him.' In other words, the way *on* is the way *in.* The way on to become more like Christ is the way in to receive Christ. Paul is not suggesting we do not need to try to be holy; in fact, active progress must be made: '*walk* in him.' Holiness, as we will see, takes effort like a walk requires the sometimes strenuous exercise of putting one foot in front of the other. But the way of holiness is not according to philosophy, human tradition, or the mystical worship of angels; it is according to Christ; it is a walk '*in him.*' Holiness is an active following of the same gospel pattern 'as you received Christ the Lord,' or as when you first became a Christian.

## *Begin Here*

So when Paul explains how practically to become more holy, he begins where we must begin: initial, real, resurrected, spiritual life. As he puts it in Colossians 3:1, 'If then you have been raised with Christ...' By saying, '*if* you have been raised with Christ,' Paul is not suggesting he has doubt in his own mind as to whether the Colossians really were Christians. He is assuming that they are. We might express it like this: '*since* you have been raised with Christ' or even 'because you have been raised with Christ.' Paul is making a logical argument: *if* that is true (which it is) *therefore* this makes sense. *If* you have been raised with Christ (which you have) *therefore* this is the right way to become more holy.

A Christian is already 'raised with Christ.' We have been raised spiritually by the resurrection power of Christ at work within us. That spiritual resurrection that has already occurred means that our coming future physical resurrection is guaranteed. But now, in the meantime, we already are spiritually raised with Christ. It is this initial, real, resurrected, spiritual life that is the *sine qua non*, the indispensable, essential, starting requirement of all real gospel holiness. You must begin here.

Without already existing spiritual life, any attempt to become holy is pointless. Worse than pointless, it can actually end up doing profound damage. It can give you the impression that you have attained some degree of holiness when in reality nothing of the sort has happened. You are merely papering over the cracks, whitewashing the tomb, covering up the spiritual decay with religious ointment. Even Jerry Bridges, who often underlined the hard work that personal holiness requires, emphasizes, 'The pursuit of holiness must be anchored in the grace of God; otherwise it is doomed to failure.'[12]

The Biblical emphasis here is brilliantly and poetically expressed in Augustine's *Confessions*:

> You called and cried out loud and shattered my deafness. You were radiant and resplendent, you put to flight my blindness. You were fragrant, and I drew in my breath and now pant after you. I tasted you, and I feel but hunger and thirst for you. You touched me, and I am set on fire to attain the peace that is yours.[13]

Or as Augustine put it more aphoristically: 'Grant what you command and command what you will.'[14]

When we are confused about holiness the primary reason is often that we misunderstand its necessary starting point. For us

---

12  Jerry Bridges, *The Discipline of Grace,* (NavPress, 2006), page 2.

13  Augustine, *Confessions*, (OUP, 1991, trans. Henry Chadwick), X.xxvii, page 201.

14  *Ibid.* X.xxix, page 202.

to please God and be more like God, more like Christ, we need to be first *raised with Christ*. So, let me ask you: have you been raised with Christ?

Consider the case of someone who grew up in a Christian home. He went to church from when he was just a baby. And yet, he began to realize that while he understood a lot about the Christian religion, he did not know what it meant to be, as Paul puts it, 'raised with Christ'. For this person it was all about doing the right thing, saying the right thing, and that was a burden he did not want to live with anymore, much less attempt to try even harder, or become holy as he thought was the definition of holiness in his own way of thinking—more effort, more rules, more religion. But he soon realized he had it the wrong way around when he came across some real Christians. He began to realize he had been trying to raise himself up when really he needed to trust in Jesus so that he could be 'raised with Christ'.

This 'being raised' is something that happens *to* you. It is something you receive. Yes, it's something you ask for—as Jesus taught, ask and you will receive (Matt. 7:7; Luke 11:9-13)—but you cannot achieve it by your own force of will, effort or endeavor. It all starts with being raised with Christ, in the power of His resurrection, by the power of His Spirit.

> 'Tis thine to cleanse the heart
> To sanctify the soul,
> To pour fresh life in every part
> And new create the whole.[15]

Ask Christ now to raise you up, make you new, give you a spiritual, resurrection-empowered, life in Him. Trust Him.

---

15    Isaac Watts, 'Come, Holy Spirit, Heavenly Dove' (1707).

Give your life to Him. Believe Him. As J.C. Ryle, the well-known evangelical Anglican Bishop and author of a renowned book on holiness called simply *Holiness*, said, 'In walking with God, a man will go just as far as he believes, and no further.'[16] Without clarifying that holiness begins with us being raised with Christ, we will tend to emphasize, as Oliver O'Donovan put it in his seminal work *Resurrection and Moral Order*, 'man taking responsibility for himself...without the good news that God has taken responsibility for him.'[17]

## *Christians are to Seek*

With this initial requirement—real spiritual life—in place, we now can be called to take the first practical step towards personal holiness: *seek*. Paul says, 'If then you have been raised with Christ, seek...' We tend to say that someone is a seeker if they are not yet a Christian (so a seeker-sensitive church usually means a church that thinks of itself as sensitive to the need to reach non-Christians). But Paul here is saying that *Christians* are to be seekers! Since we have been raised with Christ, now we are to seek; since we have new spiritual life, now we *can* seek. We are to use our regenerate will to make an effort, strenuously work, make a conscious choice, seek to be holy.

We have so often heard the evangelistic message that we need only to believe to be saved, that we have forgotten the holiness message that the saved must seek. But as J.C. Ryle said, 'It is thoroughly Scriptural and right to say "faith alone justifies." But it is not equally Scriptural and right to say "faith alone

---

16  J.C. Ryle, *Holiness*, (1879), Chapter 8, Section 4, 'Moses.'

17  Oliver O'Donovan, *Resurrection and Moral Order: An Outline for Evangelical Ethics*, (Eerdmans, 1994), page 12.

sanctifies.'"[18] Justification *is* by faith alone; sanctification is *not* by faith alone. We must seek, or make a conscious determination and effort. Becoming more holy requires the personal exertion of the Christian's regenerate will, actively seeking.

Most Christians are about as holy as they want to be. Jerry Bridges explains, 'Though the power for godly character comes from Christ, the responsibility for developing and displaying that character is ours.'[19] Christians have the power *and* the responsibility to become more holy. When you are not yet saved you cannot be holy. When you are saved now you can be holy. (And one day in heaven you will not be able to be unholy!)

A Christian, 'raised with Christ' yet still in this world, faces a battle. And the first step to winning that battle is to realize that you are in one. Meaning you must make a determination, an act of your will, to 'seek.' The great Christian leader and abolitionist William Wilberforce once said, 'No one expects to attain to the height of learning, or arts, or power...without vigorous resolution, strenuous diligence, and steady perseverance. Yet, we expect to be Christian without labor, study or inquiry.'[20] Sometimes we avoid talking about the hard work that holiness requires. Perhaps we think emphasizing the effort needed to become more holy will only put people off coming to church. We want to place the cookies on the lowest possible shelf, make Christianity like the easy button. But anything that has any value requires discipline and hard work to attain. If you want to do well at school, you must study hard. If you are going to appear

18    J.C. Ryle, *Holiness*, (1879), Section 1, 'Introduction.'

19    Jerry Bridges, *The Practice of Godliness*, (NavPress, 2008), page 55.

20    William Wilberforce, *A Practical View of the Prevailing Religious System of Professed Christians*, (Dublin, 1797), page 11.

in the city orchestra, you will need to practice your violin. If you want to perform well in the office, it will take commitment. If you want your children to do well, it requires the effort to train them.

Before you became a Christian, you did not have the spiritual power to 'seek' to become more holy. Once you are raised with Christ, now you have that spiritual power. So Paul instructs us to exercise our regenerate, born-again will and seek. Put in the effort. Work hard at it. *Seek*: you are being called to do so from God's Word. But what are we to seek?

## *Seek the Reign of Jesus*

Paul writes, '...seek the things that are above, where Christ is, seated at the right hand of God.' Paul here is probably using language drawn from the well-known Old Testament Psalm 110. That Psalm describes prophetically the victory that the Messiah will win. It is the most quoted Psalm in the New Testament. Psalm 110:1 says 'The Lord says to my Lord, "Sit at my right hand..."' Paul takes those phrases of sitting at the right hand of God to describe now the victory that Jesus won when He died, rose again, and then ascended to be with God. Christ is 'seated' at the right hand of God. He has won the victory, predicted and prophesied in Psalm 110. When Paul tells us to 'seek the things that are above,' he makes sure we understand that this 'above' place is 'where *Christ* is, seated at the right hand of God.'

To seek 'the things that are above,' then, does not mean some sort of vague looking forward to heaven after we die. It does not mean an undefined unrealistically pious way of life while on earth. To 'seek the things above' is specifically to seek Christ to rule in practice increasingly in our lives. To have the victory that He has won more and more a personal reality day by day.

Becoming more holy is essentially to seek the rule of Christ's kingdom in this world in our daily lives. But *how* are we to seek the reign of Jesus?

## *Your Mindset*

Paul tells us how in verse 2, 'Set your *minds* on things that are above, not on things that are on earth.' We seek the reign of Jesus in our daily lives by the way we 'set our minds,' by how we actively shape our thoughts, feelings, and attitudes—our whole worldview, or mindset. Holiness, then, is (rightly understood) a battle of the *mind*. It is an outworking of our true internal worldview. It is a reflection of our mindset, what we think, feel, and the attitude of our hearts. We tend to think of 'mind' as meaning something only intellectual. But Paul is writing to a recently planted church in the ancient city of Colossae, and he, of course, is not meaning by 'mind' our modern idea of IQ or school grades. He was not referring to twenty-first-century intellectual status, or mere mental assent to an idea. The 'mind' is a person's total internal approach, a mind*set* that is to shape not only schoolwork, but also homelife, work life, everyday life.

This mindset must be focused on the 'things that are above, and not on the things that are on earth.' We have already seen that the 'things that are above' refer to the reign of Christ. But what does Paul mean by 'the things that are on earth'? His definition is in verse 5: 'Put to death therefore what is earthly in you: sexual immorality, impurity, passion, evil desire, and covetousness, which is idolatry.' So the 'things that are on *earth*' (verse 2), or when he writes about 'what is *earthly* in you' (verse 5a), are 'sexual immorality, impurity, passion, evil desire, and covetousness, which is idolatry' (verse 5b).

When Paul adds 'which is idolatry,' he could be saying that all of this earthliness is idolatry. He could be saying that when our mindset is focused on this earth—'earth' as defined in verse 5—it is a sign that we have a worship problem. Or, Paul could be saying that covetousness in particular is idolatry. In either case, when Paul talks about the 'things of this earth' he is not advocating an unrealistic approach to life on this earth. Paul nowhere teaches that we are not to think about how to care for our family, how to have a good career or how to do well at school, how to be an economist or a banker or a baker, or a mom or a dad. No, by using this spatial imagery of the 'earth' below (as opposed to the things that are 'above'), Paul means things that are counter to the reign of Christ. Paul is saying that the way to be holy, to grow spiritually, is to fill our minds with what is in accord with Christ's rule rather than what is antagonistic to His rule.

This is *not* to say that merely growing in our intellectual attainment of Christian knowledge is enough. In fact, some of the most unholy people I have ever met knew quite a lot about the Bible. But that 'knowledge' had never really penetrated to shift the way they actually looked at life. We tend to say this is because what they knew in their 'head' had not penetrated to their 'heart'. But apart from being a slightly dubious biblical anthropology—a topic for a different book[21]—it disguises what is really going on. The person who acts in contradistinction

---

21  In biblical terms—I would argue this is fairly consistent across Scripture—the 'heart' is not the place of our emotions. The 'heart' is where we think, feel, and make decisions. It is the core of who we are. As one Scripture reference puts it: 'The fool says in his *heart*...' (Ps. 14:1, emphasis added). The heart is where the fool thinks, self-talks, and because of that formulates a philosophy of life.

to what he knows, does not really know it. Jonathan Edwards was at his most brilliant in this area: in what sense, Edwards would argue, does a man really know honey if he has not tasted honey? The knowledge we are talking about is one that is deeply transformative because it is genuinely experienced. The Puritans used to call it 'experimental' knowledge.

I remember one very educated man who was briefly a colleague. We had worked together on an academic course for a little while. He was an elite level professor at a city university. After we had toiled away on this project for a couple of weeks, he invited me and some friends around to show us generous hospitality. We were grateful, and we were looking forward to going with him to see his house and be with him. On the drive (it was a long distance away), he described extensively all of the effort he was putting into building his McMansion. He had yet another addition he was constructing, a swimming pool he would build, a unique design style for the aesthetics to reflect his own personality, all this and more for his perfect domestic dream. Clearly, this was where his 'mind' was 'set' and focused. After he had told us all the expense and hard work and time, I just asked him one question. What will you do when you have completed it? And to that, he had absolutely no answer.

It is easy, isn't it, for our minds to become focused on covetousness, which is really a form of idolatry? The things of this earth seem so intoxicating because they seem reasonable. Is it not better to have more? Why should I not have this experience or that sensual delight? Surely it makes rational sense to get what you can while you can.

To all this, the answer is thinking right. Listen again to the famous words of Jim Elliot: 'He is no fool who gives up that which he cannot keep to gain that which he cannot lose.'

Holiness is a battle of the mind. It is not foolish to be holy; it is wise. The solution to the siren call of earthliness is thinking accurately or rightly. The solution to covetousness is to know you are not losing out when you pursue holiness.

Holiness, the battle for holiness, starts with the mind, which means that being holy is the rational and logical thing to be. Holiness is not some masochistic, mystical nonsense. Holiness is the life that you were designed to live, what humans are meant to be. Holiness is what makes sanctified common sense, and this is why the first step in holiness is to start to put our minds back in order. If our minds are set upon being wealthy, well, what will we do when we have all that wealth?

Play golf? What then?

More golf? What then?

If our mind is set on experiencing as much sexual satisfaction as we can, what will we do when we get that? One of the strangest, if not all that surprising, truths is that there is evidence of erectile dysfunction increasing in proportion to the prominence of pornography.[22] If you ate nothing but ice cream all day, all year, soon enough, you would vomit. The founder of *Playboy Magazine* pretended to be living a life of his wildest dreams, but actually, it is reported, experienced profound sexual

---

22   'Is Internet Pornography Causing Sexual Dysfunctions? A Review with Clinical Reports,' *Behav. Sci.* (2016, 6, [3], 17; accessed April 16, 2021), https://www.mdpi.com/2076-328X/6/3/17/htm, 'Is Pornography Use Associated with Sexual Difficulties and Dysfunctions among Younger Heterosexual Men?' Alexsandar Stulhofer and Ivan Landripet, *The Journal of Sexual Medicine*, https://www.jsm.jsexmed.org/article/S1743-6095(15)31021-3/fulltext (26 March 2016; accessed April 16, 2021).

dissatisfaction.[23] There is even a demonstratable link between porn and human trafficking; when you watch porn you could be watching a coercive sex act, and by your viewership be supporting sex slavery.[24]

Paul is saying *think* about it: trace out the results of your choices and your decisions. Trace out the consequences of those earthly things, and, instead, focus on the things that are above and think about them; set your mind on them.

In many ways, the best argument for the sweetness of holiness is to meet a holy man or a holy woman. Find one. Spend time with him or her. Let the sweetness of their life logically commend to you pleasing Jesus.

I won't give away the names for the sake of avoiding embarrassing the people involved. Some time ago, a famous visiting preacher came to College Church and told me afterward of a certain 'very godly man' who had said something to him. I wondered whom he meant. When an individual came up to me later and told me that he'd said that certain something to this visiting preacher, I was amused that really, I should have guessed it was he—this 'very godly man'—who spoke to our guest. When you meet a holy man or woman you find that you are perceptibly drawn to the sweetness of that holiness.

---

23  See https://www.christianitytoday.com/ct/2003/december/hugh-hef-ners-hollow-victory.html (accessed April 8, 2021); also, http://www.breakpoint.org/2017/10/tale-two-playboys-divergent-paths-hugh-hefner-augustine-hippo/ (accessed April 8, 2021) where Hugh Hefner is said to have admitted in his later years, 'I've spent so much of my life looking for love in all the wrong places.'

24  https://www.nationalreview.com/2018/08/porn-human-trafficking-reinforce-each-other/ (accessed April 16, 2021).

Set your minds on pleasing Jesus. There is a sweetness to it. There's a joy to it. There's a freedom to it. The great problem of living a lie is that at some point or another, you are going to forget what you said to whom. It is so much less confusing to live a life of integrity. Fill your mind with the truth about Jesus. That is why I encourage good reading whenever I can. Get some books off your church bookstall or from a library or from an online store or an eBook—and read them. This is why we preach, why we train adults and children, why we have small groups around God's Word. The health and holiness of a church and an individual are inextricably correlated to what we *think* about. When we think about Jesus and have our mind filled with the truth of Jesus, we will realize that pleasing Jesus is what makes the most sense.

In other words, Paul is saying that one of the primary causes of a Christian sinning is that they are not thinking. They need to come to their senses and have their minds focused on the things that are above, on the reign of Jesus, and then they will grow spiritually. This is why we encourage one another to have a quiet time, have a devotional. This is why I spent years writing a daily devotional for people, fresh material every day explaining the whole Bible chapter by chapter, book by book. We need to be in God's Word, having our minds shaped by Truth. For out of it comes fresh new life, spiritual vitality, a focus upon the things that are above, the hope and love and joy and peace and all that Christ is and all we are in Christ, as we are raised with Christ, so we seek, an act of will, and fill our minds with the truth and with what pleases Jesus.

## The Motivation for Holiness

Well, you say that is all very well and I understand a bit more of *how* it happens: first raised with Christ, or born again, a real Christian; then seek or an act of will; and then set my mind on what pleases Jesus. Yes, I can see how, but I still don't feel very motivated. I have the *how*, but I don't yet have a *why*. Why should I be holy?

Paul concludes this first section on holiness by giving them the motivation in verses 3 and 4. He writes: 'For' [that is, this is why] 'For you have died, and your life is hidden with Christ in God. When Christ who is your life appears, then you also will appear with him in glory.'

One motivation to be holy is *who we are* as Christians. Martin Lloyd-Jones put it like this: 'The New Testament method and way of sanctification is to get us to realise our position and standing, and to act accordingly. In other words, "Be what you are."'[25] At root, at its most basic level, the motivation for holiness is a matter of identity. Who are you? If you are a Christian, Paul says, you have died; that is, by accepting Jesus as your Lord, you have died to the selfish self with all its foolish desires only to want what you want. You've died to that selfish self, and you've re-centered your life around God, around Christ. You've put to death the self in rebellion against God. That's what it means to be raised with Christ. First, you die to running your life your own way. That is what it means to be a Christian. It is who you are if you are a Christian. You have died to the selfish self. You have died. Who am I? In a certain sense, 'I'—myself—has died.

---

25 From @mljquotes, Twitter, June 8, 2021. Original citation from Iain H. Murray, *Lloyd-Jones: Messenger of Grace*, (Banner of Truth, 2008), page 222.

I am no longer on a journey to discover myself, please myself, approve of myself, and do what I like and what I want. All that has died, for Jesus is now my Lord.

But is that it? Is that all that a Christian is? No, not at all. 'You have died,' Paul says, 'and your life is hidden with Christ in God.' What a beautiful, enigmatic phrase, but what does it mean? It means that you—who you really are—is not yet fully revealed. This is how eighteenth-century commentator Matthew Henry described it:

> Our true life lies in the other world: You are dead, and your life is hid with Christ in God. The new man has its livelihood thence. It is born and nourished from above; and the perfection of its life is reserved for that state. It is hid with Christ; not hid from us only, in point of secrecy, but hid for us, denoting security.[26]

As you read this chapter, bring to your mind's eye the people in your local church. What do you see? When you look around you see this gangly, immature, teenager; or this older, wrinkled, woman; or this middle-aged man with his ill-fitting clothes; or this person with this unimpressive job, or that person with that struggling career. What do you see? There's a certain sense in which you only see the surface. The true spiritual reality is still hidden from your eyes.

There is the spiritual giant who is on his knees each night for your soul to fight through that depression that you experience. Do you see that? No. But God does.

---

26  Matthew Henry, *Commentary on Whole Bible*, Colossians 3:3. https://www.biblestudytools.com/commentaries/matthew-henry-complete/colossians/3.html Last accessed January 2022.

There is a person who seems to have life so easy, to be so successful. Yet, battles with critics and unfair accusers and learning to forgive them every single day. We may not see that. But God does.

There's the person who visits the aged and the infirmed. Do you see that? No. But God does.

There is the person who quietly gives her widow's mite into the offering plate when no one else is looking, and it is all she has to live on. Do you see that? No, but Jesus does.

There's the person who lives on only a fraction of his salary to support the work of the kingdom of God through the church. Do you see that? No. But God does.

So much of the spiritual reality of the Christian is still hidden, and therefore it is secure. When you are attacked or unfairly accused, when you are beaten down, there is a part of you—the real part of you—that no one can touch and no one can take away from you, for who you are is hidden with Christ in God. No abuser, no rapist, no bully, no murderer, no liar, no deceiver, no slanderer can take away who you are, because you are in Christ, hidden with Christ in God.

Christian, understand who you are. You are a child of God. You are an heir of the treasures of all that Christ has won in glory.

Colossians 3:4 reads, 'When Christ who is your life appears, then you also will appear with him in glory.' What an extraordinary statement!

Who am I? Christ is my life. 'When Christ who *is your life*,' think of it: *Christ* is my life! The Christian is not on a voyage of self-discovery. The Christian is on a journey of becoming more like Christ. Our task is not to discover who we are. It is to become who we were made to be. Who are you? Look to Christ.

That's who you are. Who should you be? Look to Christ. That is who you are to aim to be. *Christ is your life.*

What does that mean? Not that your individual personality is unimportant. It means that your personality becomes as it is meant to be, as you, yourself in Christ, become more like Christ. Your task is not to discover who you are, but to become who Christ made you to be. And one day, one glorious day, then you also will appear with Him in glory; not yet, then.

There's much about the Christian life now that is not glorious. We are in an arduous battle for holiness that we wage by our regenerate will, seeking to do what pleases Jesus and setting our minds on what pleases Jesus, reasoning that holiness is what makes sense. It is what is logical and truly the way we are made to live.

And Paul, therefore, gives the motivation for it all. '*For* you have died, and your life is hidden with Christ in God. When Christ who is your life appears, then you also will appear with him in glory.' What an astonishing thought! The Christian, the one raised with Christ, dies to self, rises to new life, and then when Christ returns, will share in the glory of God in Christ Jesus our Lord.

You say, 'Well, why be holy?' Because of who you are. You are Christ's. You share His life. You have this future glory to come. You are made to be this person of Christlikeness, for you are already in Christ, and your life is hid with Christ in God and you will appear with Him in glory.

Will you take a moment now to consider this? Perhaps you have not been raised with Christ. Oh, you've been to church. You know the rules, but you don't know the Ruler. Would you ask Christ to raise you up to give you new life? Pause right now and call on Christ to give you Resurrection life.

Perhaps you are a Christian, and yet, if you are being honest, you've been very passive about your holiness, your spiritual growth. And here comes God's Word and tells you to seek the things that are above. Would you make a fresh commitment to seek the reign of Jesus practically in your daily life? Write down a specific and tangible way that you can seek the reign of Jesus.

Perhaps your mind is all over the place, confused, and in a jumble. Would you ask God to help you to put your mind back into order, to have a mind that is set on Christ?

## PRAYER

*O Lord God, we thank you that, if we have been raised with Christ, our life is hid with Christ in God. We are yours. This is who we are.*

*And Lord, as we go out into this world around us, where there are countless opportunities to be distracted, innumerable videos, apps and all this media that bombard us all the time with different messages about who we are, would you help us to remember this moment, this word, of who we are as our lives are hid with Christ in God? We will appear with Him in glory. And to live life that way. To live our lives that way. To live my life that way. Lord, would you by your Spirit give us that power to do so, we pray. Would you help us to seek the things that are above? We pray this in Jesus' name. Amen.*

# 3

# *Our New Selves*

*⁵ Put to death therefore what is earthly in you: sexual immorality, impurity, passion, evil desire, and covetousness, which is idolatry. ⁶ On account of these the wrath of God is coming. ⁷ In these you too once walked, when you were living in them. ⁸ But now you must put them all away: anger, wrath, malice, slander, and obscene talk from your mouth.⁹ Do not lie to one another, seeing that you have put off the old self with its practices ¹⁰ and have put on the new self, which is being renewed in knowledge after the image of its creator. ¹¹ Here there is not Greek and Jew, circumcised and uncircumcised, barbarian, Scythian, slave, free; but Christ is all, and in all.* (Col. 3:5-11)

---

In *The Lord of the Rings* (spoiler alert), Gandalf the Grey comes back from the dead. At first, his friends do not recognize him. He has changed. He is now Gandalf the White. A Christian has also, somewhat similarly, been given a new life. We have been 'raised with Christ' (verse 1), and now 'our life is hidden with Christ in God' (verse 3). We 'have put off the old self' (verse 9), and have 'put on the new self' (verse 10). We are people made new.

But we don't always live that way. Like a drunken beggar who has been declared a prince may nonetheless for some time continue to act more beggarly than princely, a Christian can find that his previous way of life is not so easily forgotten. The Christian is indeed 'raised with Christ,' yet our old life and its habits can still exert a troubling influence over us. Less old man made new, more new man made old. How do we learn to become who we truly now are, how do we become more like our new selves?

## Spiritual Violence—Killing Sin

Paul offers a radical remedy. 'Put to death therefore what is earthly in you' (Col. 3:5). Paul is saying that the way for a Christian to grow in holiness, the way to become more spiritually mature, the way to deal with sin in our lives and to be holy, is by a process of putting sin to death. It's a kind of spiritual violence.

The great Puritan teacher, John Owen, famously said, 'Be killing sin, or sin will be killing you.'[1] You cannot take it lightly. You cannot pretend it doesn't matter. This has been the teaching of the master teachers on holiness down through the years. J. C. Ryle, famous Anglican bishop of the 19th century, emphasized that a 'holy violence'—killing sin—was necessary for spiritual growth. Ryle said that, 'A holy violence, a conflict, a warfare, a fight, a soldier's life, a wrestling, are spoken of as characteristic of the true Christian.'[2] Or again, Ryle said, 'A deep sense of that struggle, and a vast amount of mental discomfort

---

1    John Owen, *Complete Works*, vol. 6, 'The Mortification of Sin,' (Edinburgh, 1967), page 96.

2    J.C. Ryle, *Holiness*, (1879), Section 7, 'Introduction.'

from it, are no proof that a man is not sanctified. A true Christian is one who has not only peace of conscience, but war within. He may be known by his warfare as well as by his peace.'[3]

Do you know that? Do you experience that inner fight? I have found over and over again that Christians are actually greatly encouraged to know that an internal battle with sin is a characteristic sign of being a real Christian! Areas of struggle vary depending on our own individual condition. Augustine found that he could immediately give up sexual immorality once he became a Christian. But he did not find the same felicity with eating or drinking.

> Placed among these temptations, then, I struggle every day against uncontrolled desire in eating and drinking. It is not something I could give up once and for all and decide never to touch it again, as I was able to do with sexual intercourse. And so a rein has to be held upon my throat, moderated between laxity and austerity. Who is the person, Lord, who is never carried a little beyond necessity?[4]

If you were not a Christian you would not have a spiritual battle within you; the old self would not be fighting against the new self, for there would no new self for the old self to fight against. Paul is saying you must approach that fight as a fight to the death. Put sin to *death*. Holiness is a process of spiritual violence. You must kill sin. 'Put to death what is earthly in you.' Be killing sin, or it will be killing you.

You may say, I don't believe that. It's too harsh. It sounds too difficult. Haven't I been forgiven? Am I not meant to 'let go and

---

3    J.C. Ryle, *Holiness*, (1879), Chapter 2, Section 1.1, 'Sanctification.'
4    Augustine, *Confessions*, (OUP, 1991, trans. Henry Chadwick), X.xxxi, page 207.

let God'? Surely, I can find an easier path to spiritual progress. I have heard teachers who have offered me 'victory' through a little prayer, or a new spiritual experience. I prefer that path: it sounds much easier. The great missionary leader, Hudson Taylor, knew the cost it took to be holy—and the rewards. His biographer remarked, 'In these days of easy-going Christianity is it not well to remind ourselves that it really does cost—to be a man or woman God can use? One cannot obtain a Christlike character for nothing; one cannot do a Christlike work save at great price...(Phil. 3:8).'[5]

Let me put it like this. A little sin, it's only a little sin, just a small little sin, doesn't bother anyone else, it's my private little sin. Here it is—it's like a little pet sin over here, just a small little thing. A little sin is like a little poison, a little cancer. If someone said you just had a little poison in you, would you be happy to let it stay in you to kill you as it was only a little poison? If a doctor said you just had a little cancer in you, would you be happy to let it stay in you to kill you because right now it's only a little bit of cancer?

## A Little is Deadly

In Genesis 4:7, God warns Cain about the danger of sin. 'Sin is crouching at your door; it desires to have you, but you must rule over it.' The imagery is of a wild animal crouching ready to pounce and devour you.

A little sin that you feed and nourish and keep private and don't deal with and pretend that it doesn't matter very much and keep on doing it more and more—you are feeding it, nourishing it. It's like having a little pet baby lion. You keep feeding it. That

---

5    R. Steer, *Hudson Taylor: A Man In Christ*, (OMF Books, 1993), page 44.

cub is going to grow and grow, and one day it will devour you. 'Be killing sin, or it will be killing you.'

You ask, how do I do that? As we have seen, there is a precondition. You must be raised with Christ. That must happen first. This is a spiritual work. But it is also a *practical* work. Paul outlines three practical steps to putting sin to death: first develop conviction, then develop commitment, and then develop vision.

## First, Develop Conviction

The first step is to develop conviction. As J.C. Ryle long ago said, 'Men try to cheat themselves into the belief that sin is not quite so sinful as God says it is, and that they are not so bad as they really are.'[6] Conviction is not, though, being shamed or living on a guilt trip. Essentially, what we need is a gracious clarity as to the human condition, even the saved Christian condition. All of us naturally have narcissistic or selfish tendencies, exacerbated perhaps by our selfie age. But when we look in the mirror we need through the eyes of grace to discern, with loving humility, that *we* are the problem, instead of blaming other people for our problems. Apocryphally, G. K. Chesterton responded to a debate in *The Times* of London newspaper regarding what is wrong with the world by simply saying, 'Dear Sirs, What is wrong with the world? I am. Yours faithfully, G.K. Chesterton.'[7]

---

6    J.C. Ryle, *Holiness*, (1879), Chapter 1, Section 5, 'Sin.'

7    Apocryphal because this is a popular but inaccurate reference to something that Chesterton actually did write. In 1905 Chesterton wrote an essay in *The Daily News* in response to a letter written by 'A Heretic.' Chesterton's words were, 'The answer to the question, 'What is Wrong?' is, or should be, 'I am wrong.' Until a man can give that answer his idealism is only a hobby,' (*Chesterton At the Daily News*, [London, 2012], pages 167-8).

We need to have a conviction not only that sin is actually sin but that *we ourselves are actually sinning*; otherwise, we won't do anything about it.

Paul provides a precise list of particular sins. There is a laser-focused clarity to it to encourage self-assessment against a set of clear standards. It begins with 'sexual immorality.' But what does 'sexual immorality' actually mean? Is that adultery, pornography, masturbation, any kind of lust whatsoever, or what? The Greek word for 'sexual immorality' is *porneia* which in the Bible normally in this context means any kind of sexual activity outside the covenant of marriage. This is why when the woman who was caught in adultery was brought to Jesus, his question to her accusers was, 'Let him who is without sin cast the first stone'—and they all left. None of us, if we are honest with ourselves, can avoid being convicted of 'sexual immorality.' And we all need the loving Lord to say to us 'Neither do I condemn you; go then and sin no more.'

Next in Paul's list is 'impurity.' In Christian subculture when we read about 'impurity' we can think of what some have called the 'purity culture,' which has been criticized for putting unnecessary and even unfair demands upon some people. What does Paul mean by 'impurity'? In the Old Testament, the word was often used in terms of ritual purity. In the Gospels, it is quite frequently used with reference to demonic impurity or 'unclean spirits.' Paul tends to list this word next to the word sexual immorality,[8] though it appears in a wider context to indicate straightforwardness of motives in 1 Thessalonians 2:3. Obviously, here in Colossians the word impurity is right next

---

8    See, for instance, 2 Corinthians 12:21, Galatians 5:19, Ephesians 4:19, Ephesians 5:3.

to the word for sexual immorality. When Paul says 'impurity' here, then, he is indicating, with particular connection to the sexual, anything that tarnishes our life, spoils it, makes it dirty, or unclean. This idea of 'impurity' stops us from thinking of 'sexual immorality' merely in terms of body parts and functional sexual dalliance. Holiness is a broader and more beautiful attainment than simply a list of dos and don'ts. As a child, our family was given vacations in the Swiss Alps. I remember the glacier water purity of the mountain streams. Nothing is more beautiful. Similarly, we are meant to have a pure stream of the Spirit of Christ flowing in and through us. We are not to allow any impurity to muddy the beauty of holiness. Once again, who can say they are without sin?

Then, 'passion.' When we hear 'passion,' we tend to think of a strong, positive, desire. To us it means an upbeat energy towards good goals. We talk about someone having a passion for sport, or even a passion for God. However, that is not what Paul means by this word. The word for passion in Greek was originally used to describe what has happened to you whether good or bad, and as related to the soul, an experience or emotion.[9] Paul means it here as equivalent to lust, similarly to how he uses it when he writes about 'vile passions' in Romans 1:26, or the 'passion of lust' in 1 Thessalonians 4:5. To make this meaning clear, he appends to 'passion' the related category of 'evil desire'—which means both a desire that is evil and a desire for that which is evil, any sort of desire that is itself evil or is desiring something evil.

Finally, 'covetousness.' Or, to put it in more familiar language, greed. A longing for more and more, an endless pursuit of

---

9    H.G. Liddell and R. Scott, *Greek-English Lexion*, (Oxford University Press, 1996), page 1285.

temporal and material things beyond what is necessary or given graciously by God for us to enjoy.

This covetousness, Paul says, is 'idolatry.'[10] Essentially, greed is a worship problem. Greed, or covetousness, is a result of worshiping anything other than God, idolizing the creation rather than adoring the Creator. And if greed is really idolatry as Paul says, and therefore really a worship problem, how do we deal with it? By elevating who God is; that is, by worshiping God. When we enjoy God as the real God, as He truly is, we will kill the greedy desire for anything or anyone else, for we have God. What else do you need? If you are struggling with greed, you lack a big enough, exciting enough, compelling enough, vision of God. If you have God, ultimately you need nothing else. For not only does He provide what you need, He is in Himself the summation of all other desires, wants, and, yes, needs. Man does not live by bread alone but by every word that proceeds from the mouth of God.

Is it, then, by accident that an increasingly secular world is becoming more divided between the haves and the have-nots, the 1 per cent and the 99 per cent? Our culture is fueled by constant greed for more and more. 'Greed,' some even tell us, 'is good' because greed can add fuel to a consumeristic economy. Is it by accident that if church engagement decreases in a country, a greedy disparity between the rich elite and the struggling poor simultaneously increases? For we slay greed by the thrill of worship in the presence of Christ. When we together experience Christ in worship as the Lord of all and the

---

10   See discussion on page 18 for the possibility that Paul means that all these sins are expressions of 'idolatry.'

joy of all joys, we exorcize the residual plague of dissatisfaction remaining in our lives.

So, the first step to putting sin to death is to develop a conviction that sin is sinful; otherwise, we will not recognize that our little pet sin is in fact a ravenous lion that when full grown will kill us. As J.C. Ryle said, 'He that wishes to attain right views about Christian holiness must begin by examining the vast and solemn subject of sin. He must dig down very low if he would build high. A mistake here is most mischievous. Wrong views about holiness are generally traceable to wrong views about human corruption.'[11]

## *Develop Commitment*

The second step is to develop commitment. It's one thing to agree in theory; it's another thing to act. In addition to being convicted, then, we also need to develop an action plan, or real commitment, to holiness. In Colossians 3:6-8, Paul says, 'On account of these the wrath of God is coming. In these you too once walked, when you were living in them. But now you must,' note, *you must*, not you could or you may or you might, as if it were merely optional; no, *you must*, 'put them all away.'

If we ever lack commitment to put sin away, this will put backbone into the fight of any Christian: a consideration of 'the wrath of God' (verse 6). God's wrath does not mean God losing His temper or flying into a sudden and unreasonable fit of rage. The wrath of God is God's set disposition against evil, injustice, the unholy, anything that damages His creation or dishonors Him as the Creator. But Paul does not say, 'on account of these we will live suboptimal lives'; he does not say 'on account of

---

11    J.C. Ryle, *Holiness*, (1879), Chapter 1, 'Sin.'

these we will spoil our families'; he does not say 'on account of these we will miss what could have been.' All those repercussions may also be true, yet they are not where Paul focuses. He says, 'on account of these the *wrath of God* is coming.' These sins are wrath-of-God serious.

You may think, 'Well, does God have a right to be angry?' Many people wonder that today. Look at it like this. In the last few decades, many young female athletes experienced sexual abuse from an individual working for gymnastics programs across the USA. At the trial, a father momentarily lost his patience. He was shown on live TV desperately struggling to reach the abuser of his daughter to attack him. Was that father's anger understandable? Or to put it another way, should the justice system, once due process and proper investigation are completed, convict a man guilty of such heinous crimes? Should the courts deliver justice?

Let me give you another example. Recently another man has confessed to over ninety murders of socially ostracized and marginalized women working in prostitution. He targeted these women because he thought no one would care enough about them to conduct a thorough investigation. He left their remains in ditches, and it wasn't until years later that the authorities realized that it was all part of a pattern of mass murder. Let me ask you this: Should that man suffer the just consequences of his evil actions?

What about those crimes that are never judged in this world? Did Hitler, when he committed suicide, get away with it? Do you really want there to be no final justice, no wrath of God to come? The romantic idealist in us might still wish for such an unrealistic utopia. But the father of that abused daughter, the families of Jewish people put in those Nazi gas chambers, and all who have an honest view of this world as it truly can be in all its horrors, realize that justice—even the wrath of God—is good.

All sins can be forgiven when we confess them to God, repent and trust Jesus for our salvation. If you are in Christ, you are a new creation; you are not subject to the wrath of God. Paul is not saying, then, that a real Christian when he or she sins is still in danger of eternal damnation. That would run counter to Paul's theology carefully articulated in many other places, for instance, 'there is therefore now no condemnation for those who are in Christ Jesus' (Rom. 8:1). So why does Paul here write to *Christians* that it is on account of these sins that God's wrath is coming?

One early manuscript adds 'upon the sons of disobedience' to verse 6, so the full sentence would read, 'On account of these the wrath of God is coming on the sons of disobedience.' In all likelihood, the addition of 'on the sons of disobedience' was an interpretative gloss from a later scribe rather than the original that Paul wrote. But it points to the meaning. Paul is saying that these sins, that even real Christians wrestle with and must therefore put away, are the same sins as those causing so much damage in this world and are why the wrath of God is coming. To use a contemporary illustration, it's like you have received the vaccination against the Covid virus and so you yourself will not die. But you can still potentially carry the disease to infect others.

Your sin, Christian, if not put away, will not only damage others, and your own life experience too, but also is why the wrath of God is coming on the 'sons of disobedience'—your non-Christian friends, family, neighbors, and world. When you sin you are piling up reasons for God's anger to come. Which then also means that if we persist in unrepentant sin it speaks to our own lack of real spiritual life. Jonathan Edwards said it this way: 'Resolved, never to do that which I would be afraid to do were it the last thing I did in my life.'

Thomas à Kempis' famous *The Imitation of Christ* makes much of the fear of judgment. At times, it appears that he is suggesting that a real Christian, if he sins, will be purged by fire. This we cannot affirm. But we can say that if a Christian ceases to act like a Christian then he or she rightly should fear whether they really are a Christian at all—and repent. On the day of judgment, Thomas à Kempis says, 'Then he who has learned to be a fool and despised for Christ, will seem to have been wise in this world.'[12]

Or, 'Be killing sin, or sin will be killing you'—and those around you too, for the wrath of God is coming. We must commit, commit, commit to this process of spiritual violence. 'In these you too once walked,' Paul says, when you were living in that lifestyle of rebellion against God, but now you *must* put them all away.

To that end, Paul here introduces a new list that focuses on our words, not the internal life of the mind but the external divisive talk that can wreck relationships. Sins of the heart must be 'put to death' inside, in your heart and mind; these sins of words must be 'put *away*' from what you say.

I have a rule I learnt from a Christian business leader that helps me with my words. I call it 'twenty-four hours.' When I feel attacked or criticized, when I sense the desire to lash out verbally in one way or another, I will wait a full twenty-four hours. I say to myself 'twenty-four hours.' If I receive a vicious email at, say, 2pm one day, if at all possible I will avoid any kind

---

12    Thomas à Kempis, *The Imitation of Christ*, (London, 1979), page 57.

of response until it is past 2pm the next day. You might not always be able to follow that rule because some jobs use email as a mode of instantaneous interaction, but we all need to be careful with electronic communication. Don't email anything you don't want to see on the front page of the *New York Times!* You might even need to avoid any posting at all on social media. Today, many of us have to relearn that complicated relational matters are to be handled face-to-face, or at least over the phone or Zoom, not through email or WhatsApp. The rule of thumb is that the more emotional the issue the more in-person it needs to be. Another principle I learnt from a Christian leader is to never give bad news in writing. Good news in writing; bad news in person.

We can 'put away' words that cause unnecessary damage to relationships with these sorts of practical approaches. We can commit to put away 'anger', not now meaning God's wrath or His just opposition to evil, but instead the kind of intemperate cross words that damage and disconnect us from others. These angry words include 'malice'—meaning nasty, spiteful, unkind words; 'slander'—saying what is not true about someone else to damage that person's reputation; 'obscene talk from your mouth'—meaning abusive talk, all this talk here that is damaging and divisive.

Satan uses divisive talk to damage Christian relationships in an attempt to derail the mission of the church. It is serious, so serious that because of such things God's wrath is coming. I remember one person who never seemed to do anything wrong in the areas of sexual immorality, or impurity, and the like. But as we got to know him, it seemed increasingly clear that he was a gossip; a little half-truth whispered here, a bit more divisive talk dropped there. Soon enough whole groups of people were in conflict because of this man's words. I remember once literally watching him dance with joy, bop to the music that was going on in the background, when he had felt that he had managed to ruin someone's reputation. It is one of the devil's most common tactics to use the close relationships of a church to damage people through divisive talk.

If someone passes on to you a malicious rumor, say, 'Have you spoken to the person himself about that?' If divisive or damaging words are spoken about you, take comfort in the advice of the great preacher Charles Spurgeon. Remember that Spurgeon experienced extraordinary levels of brutal criticism, especially in his early years but also during the Downgrade Controversy. I am told that Spurgeon had three simple phrases he taught his ministry students to develop resilience to unfair criticism. The three phrases were these. 1) They say. 2) What do they say? 3) Let them say! People often introduce inaccurate or biased criticism with 'they say'. That phrase is used to give credibility to the criticism - 'people are saying,' 'lots of people are saying,' 'they say' - when in fact the 'they' of 'they say' almost always means just the person talking to you plus maybe one other ally or two! Spurgeon suggested we respond by frankly asking, 'what do they say?' But then shrug off the criticism with *Let them say!* Refuse to allow your peace to be disturbed by their gossip. (To balance this, we can all benefit from fair-minded criticism. Feedback from true friends and respected colleagues is a gift, even if initially painful to hear, because it is one of the best ways to learn and grow. I have heard that the British preacher Dick Lucas recommended 'the three E's of criticism': Expect it; Examine it; Endure it. But when it is divisive talk, remember Spurgeon: *Let them say!*)

There are no doubt many other ways to deal with gossip, but Paul has a bigger and more fearsome focus than mere tactics to manage unfair criticism. He is quite literally putting the fear of God into the divisive person. It is on account of slander that God's wrath is coming. Tremble lest you speak even one divisive word.

Facebook, Twitter, e-mail, WhatsApp, Instagram, TikTok, all provide opportunities for instantaneous communication to vast numbers of people. They magnify and multiply speech, for good or ill. The potential for gossip has never been greater. All these media tools can be used to disseminate the message of Christ, but they can also spread a viral contagion of divisive and damaging talk. During the social distancing introduced by governments in the Covid-19 pandemic, people used social media to build connections, encourage and inform others— when corporate gatherings were so limited. Social media makes an excellent tool when used for these purposes. However, people can utilize the same Internet technologies to become cowardly slanderers hidden behind a keyboard. What is the line from those superhero movies? Stan Lee coined the phrase: 'With great power comes great responsibility.' Each of us with a phone today has great power. There is more computing RAM in one of those phones than was used to send a man to the moon! You can communicate with thousands of people at the touch of a button. Commit, would you commit, to putting away divisive speaking, texting and typing, slander of whatever kind?

## *Developing Vision*

The third step is to develop a positive vision for the end results of our holiness. We can so often view holiness as something negative, unpleasant and unenjoyable. But that view of holiness is quite unbiblical. We are to kill sin not be a kill-joy! After all, the fruit of the Spirit is joy. And when we pursue holiness there is an end result which is enormously positive for the experience of the Christian community of the church, both as individuals within that community and for the body as a whole. So in verses 9 through 11, Paul says, 'Do not lie to one another, seeing that you have put off the old self with its practices and have put on the new self, which is being renewed in knowledge after the image of its creator. Here there is not Greek and Jew, circumcised and uncircumcised, barbarian, Scythian, slave, free; but Christ is all, and in all.'

When Paul says 'here,' what is he thinking about? Where is 'here'? It is this 'new self,' but as he describes the 'new self' he slips over from the individual to the communal. Here, with the new self, there is not Greek or Jew, circumcised and uncircumcised, barbarian, Scythian, slave, free—all these divisions that plagued the ancient world, Scythians being despised by the Greeks—but now Christ is all, and is in all. The 'here' is the united, loving, barrier-breaking, new self of the community of the church. Here we are not to lie to each other or spread divisive talk. Here we are renewed by God's Word more into the image of our Creator. Here is a community of different races and classes all united in Christ. A biblical vision of church is the true expression of that famous longing for a better world that John Lennon so memorably sung in 'Imagine.' We could reword his famous lyrics to capture a New Testament vision of community around the gospel:

*Imagine—it's easy if you can - a place where people of all colors live as one.*

*Imagine a place where a billionaire holds hands with a pauper.*

*Imagine a place where border guards embrace the children of refugees.*

*Imagine...the New Testament vision of church!*

Paul is trying to help us see what becoming more like Christ will do. Christ is the one in whom all these divisions—Jews and non-Jews, barbarians, and Scythian, the uncivilized and the civilized, the uncultured and the cultured, slave or free—all these divisions are broken down. And as we who follow Christ are renewed by the 'knowledge' of God's Word, as we stop lying and stop speaking divisive words, so we become more holy and so the church is transformed into being more like Christ. By pursuing the real nature of gospel holiness, the community of the church is gradually transformed. The wolf can lie down with the lamb. The estranged father with the embittered daughter. The grandchild with the grandmother. The beloved prodigal is embraced in the all-encompassing love of the Father, and the older brother no longer scowls but now rejoices too. This, Paul is saying, is what holiness does. Becoming like Christ. In community. Together. *Here,* in church.

Imagine a family, a church, a school, a community, a world ruled by the King of all kings, the Lord Jesus Christ. And so, put off sin for this dream, this vision, of the new community of Christ.

If you are a small group leader, your commitment to studying the Bible in private will be the example that helps shape your small group around the Bible. If you are a student leader, your commitment to private prayer will help raise a generation of teenagers who become prayer warriors who follow your example. If you are a deacon or elder, your commitment to personal generosity will help build a healthy budget. If you are an attendee or member of a church, your commitment to speak the truth and avoid divisive talk will help form a healthy community. If you are a mother or child, a father or grandfather, as you develop a conviction about sin, a commitment to put sin to death, your growing Christlikeness will do more to bless your family than anything else you could possibly do. It's that big a vision, and it makes that much difference and the stakes are that high. As one Puritan prayed:

> Cause me to be a mirror of thy grace, to show others the joy of thy service... Help me to walk as Jesus walked, my only Savior and perfect model, his mind my inward guest, his meekness my covering garb.[13]

Will you catch this vision of the difference it would make if you are convinced and committed to put sin in your life to death? We are talking about relational reconciliation. We are talking about people from different races getting along. We are talking about families being rebuilt, and it comes down to your taking Paul's call here to put sin to death seriously. Holiness is fueled by conviction, commitment, but also by this vision of the difference that it makes in the real world through the New Testament church. Essentially, the reason why the church—and by extension the church's influence on the world—is so fragmented, and we are so divided, is not because Christ is insufficient to reconcile. The reason is that we who are Christians are not becoming more holy. Any residual racism

---

13    Arthur Bennet, *The Valley of Vision*, (Edinburgh, 1975), page 136.

and classism and prejudice in church are a sign of our lack of Christlikeness. Therefore: be holy!

## Encouragement

Before we leave this section, though, I want to encourage you. Don't give up! It can feel as if you're never going to be good enough. You can feel ashamed when you fail—yet again. But remember: holiness is a *process*. There is no immediate victory, no sudden effortless Christlikeness. Holiness is a path to follow, a process to commit to. It requires patient, and also often painful, plodding, perseverance. If you feel like you are only making gradual progress, you're not alone. That is the nature of holiness. It takes time. It's more like climbing a mountain than flipping a switch. As you walk there are times when you feel you are making progress, and then there are times when you seem to be going back down again, but in Christ gradually the overall progress is up. Listen to how Jerry Bridges expressed it in *The Pursuit of Holiness*:

> Learning this [the gradual progress of holiness] is usually a slow and painful process fraught with many failures. Our old desires and sinful habits are not easily dislodged. To break them requires persistence often in the face of little success, but this is the path we must tread, painful though it may be.[14]

Why is this clear-eyed perspective of the process of holiness encouraging? Because it gives us a long-term view, which strengthens us to keep going and not give up when there are difficulties along the way. You and I are to commit to this process and persist in it *even when we fail.* A mark of a godly man or woman is not unrealistic perfectionism; it is a stick-it-out-

---

14    Jerry Bridges, *The Pursuit of Holiness* (NavPress, 2006), page 74.

ness, keep-on-going-ness, gradual improvement in the process of holiness, despite even perennial and dogged failures. As the book of Proverbs says, a righteous person is one who falls down many times, but he *stands up again*.[15] You've fallen down? Stand up. Commit to the process. Put off the old self (again).

## *Equipping*

But not only do I want to encourage you, I also want to equip you. Start by asking yourself the simple question, 'How can I make progress in holiness?' What do I need to do differently, or more frequently—or less often? What changes should I make, what habits should I encourage? Take a clear look at your own life, in the light of this process of conviction and commitment and vision, and see if you can prayerfully determine what needs to change.

Many times, the key comes down to the most simple habit of all: what some Christians call 'the quiet time,' and other Christians call 'daily devotions.' I never cease to be amazed at how often even quite experienced Christians ignore, or downplay, the importance of a personal, daily habit of reading the Bible and praying. One missionary leader, when he discovered that a missionary had had a moral failing, would always ask his team 'when did he stop having quiet times?' The question was not '*did* he stop having quiet times?' but '*when* did he stop having quiet times?' My pastoral experience is similar: I have never yet met anyone who has had a significant moral failing who at the same time has been enjoying deep daily fellowship with Christ. Of course, Jesus teaches us this in His famous metaphor of the vine and the branches. 'I am the vine; you are the branches,'

---

15    Proverbs 24:16

Jesus said, 'Whoever abides in me and I in him, he it is that bears much fruit, for apart from me you can do nothing' (John 15:5).

Ensure that you spend time in prayer. Don't let your schedule become so packed that you have no time for God. First thing in the morning, or if you are a parent of young children maybe after the children have gone to school, or last thing at night—one way or another—make sure you have time for a heart-to-heart conversation with your Father.

Read the Bible too, but in an expectant and lingering way. It's not a quick shower; it's a bath. Meditate on the words you are reading in your Bible passage. Christian meditation is the lost art of taking a Bible text and churning it over in your mind until by the Spirit it penetrates deep within. Meditate on Colossians 3.

As we do, as we follow the process of conviction and commitment, the beautiful vision of multicolored Christocentric unity starts to come into view in the community of the church. We are neither Greek nor Jew, neither slave nor free. Not barbarian nor Scythian, old, young, rich, poor. Christ is all and is in all.

## PRAYER

*Our Lord Jesus, we do bow before you and pray that would be the case. We pray, Christ, that you would rule in our hearts and minds individually and as a church community. We pray, Lord Jesus, that your rule would extend to those around us. And we pray, Lord, that as that happens increasingly there will be joy, and we ask these things in Jesus' name. Amen.*

# 4
# Getting Dressed

*¹² Put on then, as God's chosen ones, holy and beloved, compassionate hearts, kindness, humility, meekness, and patience, ¹³ bearing with one another and, if one has a complaint against another, forgiving each other; as the Lord has forgiven you, so you also must forgive. ¹⁴ And above all these put on love, which binds everything together in perfect harmony. ¹⁵ And let the peace of Christ rule in your hearts, to which indeed you were called in one body. And be thankful. ¹⁶ Let the word of Christ dwell in you richly, teaching and admonishing one another in all wisdom, singing psalms and hymns and spiritual songs, with thankfulness in your hearts to God. ¹⁷ And whatever you do, in word or deed, do everything in the name of the Lord Jesus, giving thanks to God the Father through him.* (Col. 3:12-17)

---

In the *Harry Potter* world you can take Polyjuice potion to transform yourself into a different person. It is important to have clothes ready to fit the shape of your new body. And if you change back again before you have a chance to put on your old attire, you could end up wearing something that was ridiculously too small or large. Likewise, part of our growing up to be an adult is learning to put on clothes that fit. We learn how to get dressed in the morning. We develop the ability to choose clothes that suit our bodies as well as are appropriate for different occasions. We don't dress in clothes that are much too small or big; we don't wear a swimsuit at a wedding, or formal evening garb at a beach party. We put on clothes that at least roughly match our physical contours and the social situation.

Paul is instructing the Colossians to 'put on' characteristics that fit who they now are (verse 12). As we have seen earlier, we must first be 'raised with Christ' to become a new person (verse 1). Paul then taught us to 'put off' our previous way of life (verse 9). Now Paul is saying we 'put on' a new set of clothes. A holy man is a sharp dressed man.

A year or so ago I was fairly sick over the summer. I lost quite a lot of weight. Afterwards, I remember looking at my clothes and beginning to try them on. The belt buckle needed to be tightened several notches. The shirts were too loose. Clothes I had not been able to wear since I was young and svelte, I could now again just about squeeze into!

The change you have been through if you have become a Christian is far more radical than losing some weight. You are 'chosen', 'holy' and 'beloved' (verse 12). You are chosen: God picked you. You are holy: God has set you apart for His purposes. You are beloved: God passionately cares for you. Now, put on clothes that match this gospel reality. Wear what suits you now. Put on the wardrobe of Christ. Put on the new clothes that fit the new you.

All this means that the Christian approach to character development is not the same as ancient Stoicism—or its contemporary form as articulated (in various ways) by people like David Brooks or Jordan Peterson. David Brooks' book

*The Road to Character*[1] is—I hesitate for fear of overstating—
one of the more important books written in recent years. He
is articulating a massive, under-taught, under-appreciated,
desire for consistent character. Years ago, the psychologist
M. Scott Peck said something similar in his famous tome *The
Road Less Travelled.*[2] He opined that America needed a 'statue
of responsibility' on the West Coast to balance the Statue
of Liberty on the East Coast. There is a market for modern
forms of scientifically sophisticated stoicism. Jordan Peterson's
phenomenally successful *12 Rules for Life* shows as much.[3] He
works out from evolutionary biology (consider the lobster) to
practical techniques (first clean your room). His argument is
that given the hardwired nature of hierarchies in evolutionary
biology, it is important that every sentient being—from lobster
to human—learns to stand up straight and take responsibility.
And all this is, in many ways, good. New Testament scholars
have long batted back the accusation that Paul's list of virtues
is 'merely' stoic. But there is an important difference between
Christian and—whether ancient or modern—stoicism. The
difference is that a Christian has become a new person. The
Christian task is not to develop their character by iron will.
The Christian task is to put on the characteristics of Christ
that match who Christ has made them now to be. While we
can learn from those—like Brooks and Peterson—who call us
towards a contemporary stoicism, without the transforming
power of Christ we do not have the resources to become who

---

1    David Brooks, *The Road to Character*, (Random House, 2015).

2    M. Scott Peck, *The Road Less Travelled*, (Arrow Books, 1978).

3    Jordan Peterson, *12 Rules for Life: An Antidote to Chaos*, (Random
     House, 2018).

we are made to be. Ultimately, it's a dead end, one which only the resurrection power of Christ can overcome.

## *The Clothes of Christ*

Paul wants us to wear spiritual clothes that reflect the reality that we are a rescued people, a forgiven people, who did not receive what we deserved. Paul provides a list of merciful and grace-filled characteristics that he wants us to 'put on.'

It starts with 'compassionate hearts'—an internal feeling that is moved by the plight of the weak and troubled. Christians are not hardened towards others. We know what it is like to be in difficulty ourselves. When we see someone stumble, our instinct is to feel sympathy, empathy, and compassion because we know what it is to be stuck in sin and need saving.

'Kindness'—with that internal feeling of compassion, then comes the action that follows, namely 'kindness.' This kindness is a Spirit-produced generosity that is not harsh but instead cares for the thriving of other people. Like the Good Samaritan, a Christian is not merely to feel compassion but to enact a practical care plan.

'Humility'—perhaps the rarest of virtues in our self-asserting age. It is also one of the most precious. Humility is a true perspective about our own gifts and character that comes from a realistic recognition of what we were before God saved us. We no longer compare ourselves with other people. We look to God and His grace and are humbled. Humility is not low self-esteem. Humility is a realistic appraisal of what we are good at, as well as what we are not good at. A truly humble person is free from codependency and peer pressure. He or she is no longer controlled by what people think, but now lives for what God wants and is, therefore, able to live as God designed them to live.

Humility is the alchemy of healthy community; without it there is little chance of unity.

'Meekness'—people often think of meekness as meaning weakness, but the biblical idea combines gentleness with strength. A meek person is a person who has great power, but that power is under control. A meek horse is a warhorse that has been trained not to be frightened by the sounds of war. And a meek man or woman is a person who has power under the control of God's Spirit. As a saved person, with the Spirit of Christ within them, they now channel their energy towards God-given goals. They don't lash out and live chaotic lives. They are disciplined and focused, and, well, meek.

'Patience'—this is not merely being begrudgingly willing to wait a long time when queuing or standing in line at a grocery store. A patient person is someone who has a long fuse, does not easily become angry or upset, does not have a short temper. They overlook an offense. They are not quick to rise up in passionate anger. God is patient with them, and so they are patient with others.

And then in verse 13, Paul emphasizes the principle that motivates all these characteristics, namely God's forgiveness of us. He says, '...bearing with one another and, if one has a complaint against another, forgiving each other; as the Lord has forgiven you, so you also must forgive.' Because we are *forgiven* people, Christians are to *forgive* people.

The chief and primary barrier to forgiving other people is an overestimation of our own righteousness and an underestimation of our own forgiveness.

Let me show you how that works through a powerful story of real forgiveness:

Betsie and I had been arrested for concealing Jews in our home during the Nazi occupation of Holland. This man had been a guard at Ravensbruck concentration camp where we were sent.

Now he was in front of me, hand thrust out: 'A fine message, Fraulein! How good it is to know that, as you say, all our sins are at the bottom of the sea!'

And I, who had spoken so glibly of forgiveness, fumbled in my pocketbook rather than take that hand. He would not remember me, of course—how could he remember one prisoner among those thousands of women?

But I remembered him and the leather crop swinging from his belt. I was face-to-face with one of my captors and my blood seemed to freeze.

'You mentioned Ravensbruck in your talk,' he was saying. 'I was a guard there.' No, he did not remember me.

'But since that time,' he went on, 'I have become a Christian. I know that God has forgiven me for the cruel things I did there, but I would like to hear it from your lips as well. Fraulein,'— again the hand came out—'will you forgive me?'

And I stood there—I whose sins had again and again to be forgiven—and could not forgive. Betsie had died in that place—could he erase her slow terrible death simply for the asking?

\* \* \*

And still I stood there with the coldness clutching my heart. But forgiveness is not an emotion—I knew that too. Forgiveness is an act of the will, and the will can function regardless of the temperature of the heart. 'Jesus help me,' I prayed silently. 'I can lift my hand. I can do that much. You supply the feeling.'

And so woodenly, mechanically, I thrust my hand into the one stretched out to me. And as I did, an incredible thing took place. The current started in my shoulder, raced down my arm, sprang into our joined hands. And then this healing warmth seemed to flood my whole being, bringing tears to my eyes.

'I forgive you, brother!' I cried, 'With all my heart.'[4]

Corrie Ten Boom learned to forgive. Will you? Will you 'stretch out your hand' too? If you do, it will require putting on love, for it is love that beautifully binds all these other clothes together. Paul says, 'Above all these put on love, which binds everything together in perfect harmony' (Col. 3:14). Love is the ultimate Christian virtue, for it holds together all others in perfect harmony. You are loved. You are 'chosen,' you are 'beloved' (verse 12); therefore, 'put on love' (verse 14).

What is love? Love is the expression of all these other virtues. It is patient. It is kind. It keeps no record of wrongs. Love is the harmonious music that orchestrates all the Christlike actions of the Christian. It is not a mere sentiment. It is doing what is in the best interest of other people for the glory of God.

We are putting on these new clothes, these clothes of the characteristics of Christ. We are putting on this wardrobe of new clothes that fit who we now are in Christ. The power for all this is the risen power of Christ by His Spirit. We are a new creation. We now need a new set of clothes that fit who we really are. And Paul is listing what these new clothes are, and we're defining them and applying them to our own lives. We are calling ourselves to put on the clothes of Christ, all bound together by the love of Jesus. And next Paul moves on to show us how these characteristics of Christ are not 'solos' but are harmoniously orchestrated as the church.

---

4    *Tramp for the Lord* (Revell, 1974), pages 56-57.

## The Body of the Church

So in Colossians 3:15-17, Paul says, 'And let the peace of Christ rule in your hearts, to which indeed you were called in one body. And be thankful. Let the word of Christ dwell in you richly, teaching and admonishing one another in all wisdom, singing psalms and hymns and spiritual songs, with thankfulness in your hearts to God. And whatever you do, in word or deed, do everything in the name of the Lord Jesus, giving thanks to God the Father through him.'

We are, then, to 'let' the 'one body' of the church be clothed with these characteristics of Christ through Christ's peace, Christ's Word, and Christ's name.

Christ's peace, verse 15. 'Let the peace of Christ rule in your hearts.' Christ's peace is not a sentimental feeling of peace. Christ's peace is the objective peace that Christ's death on the cross has achieved. That peace is to rule over the one body of the church. In church, then, the rule of what I want is to be replaced by the rule of what Jesus wants. And so we have peace. We submit to the peaceful rule of King Jesus, not fight with the divisive monster of endlessly squabbling factions of King Self. As the great missionary leader Hudson Taylor put it, 'The real secret of an unsatisfied life lies too often in an unsurrendered will.'[5]

One week I didn't check my email for two whole days. By the end of those two days, my in-box had 300 unanswered emails. Some of them were junk or spam, no doubt. Most of them encouraging and pleasant to read, but each of them had their own expressed preference about this, that, or the other. It's not

---

5    J. Hudson Taylor, *Union and Communion*, (Ichthus Publications, 2017), page 12.

wrong to have our own point of view on something. It *is* wrong to insist on our view to the damage of others in the one body. Instead, we must let the body be clothed with the rule of Christ's peace.

We do that through Christ's Word, verse 16. 'Let the word of Christ dwell in you richly....' So, if the *crown* or 'rule' of the *body* of the church is Christ's peace, Paul, now switching metaphors but still focusing on community, shows us how the *riches* of the *dwelling* of the house of the church is Christ's Word. Letting the Word of Christ dwell in us richly or abundantly or thoroughly or completely means the message of the Bible about Jesus filling every room in the house with the treasures of the gospel.

This means Biblical preaching. In our individualistic and sentimental age, we tend to downplay the spiritual efficacy of listening to biblical preaching. Our forebears understood. As the First London Confession succinctly summarized, 'Faith is ordinarily begotten by the preaching of the gospel, or the word of Christ....'[6] Or as Question 155 of the Westminster Catechism elaborated: 'How is the word made effectual to salvation? The Spirit of God makes the reading, but especially the preaching of the word, an effectual means of...establishing their hearts in holiness and comfort through faith unto salvation.'[7]

It also means meditating on Scripture in our own quiet times. It means each of us, not just full-time paid ministers, but each of us teaching one another the Word, in larger groups and smaller groups and one-to-one discipleship, discipling a younger Christian, asking someone to disciple you. It means telling our friends about this Word of Christ, inviting people to

---

6    *First London Confession*, 1646, Article XXIV.

7    *Westminster Larger Catechism*, 1647, 155.

come to church. It means admonishing one another in wisdom, that is, asking for God's gracious wisdom to remind each other of the Word of Christ.

It means 'singing psalms and hymns and spiritual songs.' *Singing* is an important ministry of the Word. A wide variety of different types of singing is to be all filled with the treasures of Christ too. As one commentator said, 'What the apostle is concerned about is that these songs are consistent with the Word of Christ. Genuine Christian praise is a celebration of God's mighty acts in Christ.'

Christ's peace through Christ's Word and all in Christ's name: 'Whatever you do, do it all in the name of the Lord Jesus' (Col. 3:17). Everything then is to be guided by the principle of the name. Can this be done in Jesus' name? If we cannot say something or do something in a way that reflects what Jesus would say or do, then we should not say it or do it. By the rule of Christ's peace, through the riches of Christ's Word, by the principle of Christ's name, we 'put on' Christ now in the community of the church, the one body, the house under Christ's rule.

In some parts of America there are many churches, and it is easy—all too easy—in those areas to think of church in consumeristic terms. You go to this church because of this kind of program, or another church because it has a different approach and, in making these preferential choices, you can end up missing out on real church. Going to church gets real when you don't get what you want! It is then that we find out what church is all about, which is not our individual preferences but being one body ruled by Christ's peace through His Word and all in His name.

In addition, Paul has a simple method to lubricate the sometimes creaking joints of this one body of the church. He repeats it three times: verse 15, 'Be thankful,' verse 16, '...with thankfulness in your hearts to God,' and verse 17, '...giving thanks to God the Father through him.' The oil of thanksgiving keeps the joints of a church healthy, while grumbling is rust and corrosion.

How can we become more holy? As we have seen, it begins with spiritual power, that is, being raised with Christ—asking Christ to raise you up to make you born again. Holiness is a spiritual work. But it is also deeply practical. Jerry Bridges said, '[Holiness] is a joint venture between God and the Christian. No one can attain any degree of holiness without God working in his life, but just as surely no one will attain it without effort on his own part.'[8] We must put off the clothes that no longer fit us as Christians, and put on these other clothes that now do fit us as Christians. And we do this in the community of the church, the one body to which we are called by being thankful, so having Christ's peace rule through His Word and in His name.

## Four Application Steps

First, make a list of things about which you can be thankful. Write them down. Put the list on your fridge. Put it in the back of your Bible. Once you start giving thanks, it is amazing how it changes your attitude to other people in the church.

Second, identify one of these virtues that you know you need to put on and target it specifically. Is it patience? Is it forgiveness? This week, you can grow in holiness by asking God to help you

---

8    Jerry Bridges, *The Pursuit of Holiness,* (NavPress, 1978), page 10.

put on one of these virtues in particular. If you cannot think of one, then I suggest humility!

Third, go to church, not with an attitude of resistance or reluctance, but an attitude of receptivity. Let the peace of Christ rule and the Word of Christ dwell in you richly. Before you walk in the church door, breathe a silent prayer to yourself, 'Lord, what do you want to teach me today?' Before I go to church, I talk to God about the things that are on my mind, but then having done that, I change focus to listen to God by saying, 'Lord, tell me what it is that you want me to hear this morning.'

Fourth, apply the rule of the name, that whatever you do in word or deed, do it in the name of the Lord Jesus. If you cannot send that email with a signature at the bottom, 'Love, Jesus,' do not send it. If you cannot write that blog with the name at the bottom, 'From the Lord Jesus,' do not write that blog. If you cannot say that to your family or church member by saying, 'This is what Jesus says in the Bible,' do not say it. If you can bless someone, love someone, encourage someone, lift up someone, alleviate someone's burdens, forgive someone, all these things in the name of the Lord Jesus, then say it, do it.

## PRAYER

*Our Lord Jesus, I ask that you would raise up those who do not yet have spiritual new life. Would You do that by the power of your Spirit? Would you graciously have mercy on them? Would you raise them up to give them the spiritual power they need to follow you? Would You release them from legalism and condemnation, and show them how much You love them? Would You raise them up by your Spirit? I plead with you. Would you do that, Lord Jesus?*

*And Father, I pray for all of us who know you and are loved by you and know that in truth. Lord, would you help us to put* on these characteristics of Christ? Would you help us to target one specifically?

And Lord, I pray for the church as a body, the one body, that Your peace would rule through your Word, and that we together, giving thanks, would do all things in the name of Jesus in whom we pray. Amen.

# 5
# Home and Work

*18 Wives, submit to your husbands, as is fitting in the Lord. 19 Husbands, love your wives, and do not be harsh with them. 20 Children, obey your parents in everything, for this pleases the Lord. 21 Fathers, do not provoke your children, lest they become discouraged. 22 Bondservants, obey in everything those who are your earthly masters, not by way of eye-service, as people-pleasers, but with sincerity of heart, fearing the Lord. 23 Whatever you do, work heartily, as for the Lord and not for men, 24 knowing that from the Lord you will receive the inheritance as your reward. You are serving the Lord Christ. 25 For the wrongdoer will be paid back for the wrong he has done, and there is no partiality.*

*4 Masters, treat your bondservants justly and fairly, knowing that you also have a Master in heaven.* (Col. 3:18–4:1)

---

When I teach on this passage, I am reminded of the son who did not want to attend church. He hid up in his room. His mother called to him. 'It's time to go to church!' He refused to come downstairs. 'It's time!' his mother shouted again. He bellowed back, 'I don't want to go. I have no friends. No one likes me!' 'You have to,' his mother responded. 'Why?' He said. 'Because,' his mother insisted, 'you're the pastor and you're preaching!' Joking aside, I doubt there are many pastors who relish preaching on this particular passage today.

And yet we must address these most practical areas of personal holiness. If holiness does not impinge on the domestic, the economic, the private and the public, of what use is it? The Bible is unabashed in teaching holiness in these areas. Home and work, work and home, holy here, holy there, holy everywhere!

## 1. A Message for Wives

Verse 18 starts with a message for wives.[1] 'Wives, submit to your husbands, as is fitting in the Lord.' I want you to notice that this verse is not directed to husbands. It does not say, 'Husband, tell your wife to submit to you.' So, husband, do not jump up now and say to your wife, 'Hey, the Bible says submit to me; therefore, I command you to...go and do the dishes,' and blame the explosion your words will create on my exposition! That kind of finger-wagging lecturing is not what the Bible is teaching. This verse is not a patriarchal power move. Husbands are not fathers (that's what the word 'patriarch' means, father-rule) to their wives; they are husbands to them. This verse was not meant to browbeat your wife and bully her into submission. None of that is what Paul is intending. It is not the right way to use this text.

But I also want you to observe the key emphasis of Paul in this passage. He says, 'As is fitting in the Lord.' It is a condition that runs throughout these six instructions: 'in the Lord,' 'as is fitting in the Lord.' Remember, throughout Colossians chapter 3 Paul is teaching the spiritual necessity of being 'raised with

[1] A good resource for further reading is Claire Smith's *God's Good Design: What the Bible Really Says About Men and Women*, (Matthias Media, 2012).

Christ' (3:1) to all real gospel holiness. Now once more Paul evokes the person and power of Jesus by repeatedly referring to Him: '... as is fitting in the *Lord*...for this pleases the *Lord*... fearing the *Lord*...serving the *Lord Christ*...you also have a *Master* in heaven.'

Whatever you decide these instructions mean for your home and work, they must match the pattern of who Jesus is— as is 'fitting in the Lord.' So Paul cannot mean that a wife must do whatever her husband says without any exceptions. After all, a husband might tell his wife to do something plain wrong or sinful, push her around even abuse her. But immoral, much less evil, demands are not 'fitting in the Lord.' This Christocentric clarification is especially important today because the word 'submit' is often misunderstood. Many assume that the word 'submit' means to be subjugated by, controlled by, under the thumb of, dominated by someone else. But none of that is 'fitting in the Lord.' That is not how Jesus treats us; it does not fit the Christ-pattern.

At the same time, we also cannot allow contemporary secular sensitivities to overrule biblical parameters. Nowadays, many people feel the very idea of 'submission' is abhorrent in almost all circumstances. Even in a work scenario, most would be unlikely to sign a contract that said we must 'submit' to our boss. Perhaps the military service chain of command comes closest to an acceptable contemporary context for what we think Paul means by 'submission' here.

But what did Paul actually mean? The word 'submit' indeed has a sense of placing yourself under someone else.[2] However,

---

2   'Place or arrange under,' H.G. Liddell and R. Scott, *Greek-English Lexicon,* (Oxford University Press, 1996), page 1897.

that does not imply that the one submitting has no rights, nor that there is no responsibility on the other side of the relationship. One reason why we find the biblical idea about submission hard to grasp is partly because we tend to accentuate leadership not followership. There is a whole leadership industry today. As far as I know there is no followership industry! Additionally, one of the anomalies of current Western society is our difficulty with believing that power is anything but potentially bad. Power corrupts, in the familiar phrase, and absolute power corrupts absolutely. Power, we tend to think, is intrinsically evil. But what about God's power? Is good power possible? Is it in your best interests to submit to someone who loves you enough to die for you?

Perhaps it will be helpful to offer the kind of advice that Rochelle and I have given for years when we have done premarital counseling. The relationship of marriage is a two-sided coin. It is almost impossible to submit to someone who does not care about you—or at least to do so in anything but a begrudging way, not from the heart. But it is not that hard to submit to someone who is truly giving up his life for your best. Submission of the wife requires self-sacrifice of the husband. It can only work when there is a duality. It is also an art: the idea of a husband telling his wife what to do without being in conversation with her is, to me, absurd. Who could be such an idiot? But unfortunately, bitter pastoral experience teaches me that many men are precisely that idiotic. She is made in the image of God! She is remade in the image of Christ! Read Proverbs 31! Do you really think that her submitting to you means you get to do whatever you want? How ridiculous.

I also need to speak a word about the boundaries of this submission. Nowhere in the Bible does it teach that all women should submit to all men. Relational gender role duality is carefully subscribed to only two areas in the Bible: marriage, and the local church. I certainly don't want to stir up another hornet's nest by talking about roles of men and women in church, but it's important to understand the biblical logic. The reason why men and women play different roles in marriage *and* in church is because the church is the bride of Christ: church is the real marriage. Marriage is intended to be a role drama of Christ giving up His life for the church. When you look at a healthy Christian marriage, what you should see is an enacting of Christ's sacrifice and the church's following being played out before your eyes. A healthy marriage should feel like love and reception, grace and faith, death and life, Jesus and the church. By playing these roles, the married partners together send a message. Your marriage is a pulpit, indeed the most significant pulpit (preachers take note) you will ever have.

The kind of theology being taught here, sometimes called 'complementarianism,' is at times accused of being psychologically unhealthy. But the sad truth is that people can twist any theology, or philosophy, to their own ends. I've certainly known of people who hide behind a theology of complementarianism to act out fantasies of abusive power manipulation. But I've also known of people who employ the contrasting theology, sometimes called 'egalitarianism,' for the same nefarious purpose. One massively influential, egalitarian church had a leader who was accused of mistreating the women on his staff. I'm sure the same can happen in complementarian churches too. It's a bit like that old debate as to whether extremist right-wingers or left-wingers are better or worse; to be in the Gulags under Stalin or in the concentration camps under

Hitler was bad either way. The wickedness of the human heart devastates—and grabs hold of different theories to do so.

The real sweat and sweetness of marriage is worked out away from the posturing and posing that often goes under the guise of much so-called ideological sophistication—in the bedroom, in the hospital room, in the kitchen. My instinct is that all healthy Christian marriages actually operate as Paul here indicates, even if they use different theological labels. I've known supposed 'egalitarian' marriages that to me look very like what Paul describes. I've also known professed 'complementarian' marriages that look nothing like what Paul describes. And vice versa.

How then does this verse about submission work in practice? Taking my courage in both hands, let me make a few suggestions. Wives, remember that your husband longs to be respected. Women need to be respected too, of course. And a man's need for respect is no excuse for him to be a baby. But how many women truly understand the power of honoring their man? I have learnt over the years that the number two predictor (I could tell you more about the number one another time: reading the Bible personally and regularly) of a husband's spiritual vitality is the wise supportiveness of his wife. If a husband feels that for at least his wife he is a hero—well, that man will rise to otherwise unforeseen heights of greatness. That's the power you have, wives. Don't abandon it because it's unfashionable to use it.

Now, before we move on, a word about the hard cases. What if you are married to a man for whom there is very little that you can, as a Christian, in good conscience respect? What do you do then? Start with remembering the framework Paul gives when he says, 'As is fitting in the Lord.' God is not asking you to pretend that your man is what he is not, nor is he asking you to submit to things that are ungodly or unwise or not 'fitting in the Lord.' If you face trauma or crisis in your marriage, I encourage you to talk to a pastor and prayerfully seek specific godly counsel. Do not rely on generic (however well-intentioned) instructions that you might glean from searching on the internet. As Tolstoy famously wrote, 'Happy families are all alike, but every unhappy family is unhappy in its own way.'[3] Paul here is showing how a happy, godly family works. When that family breaks down it can shatter in any number of ways. A beautiful vase of a godly family forms a certain Christlike pattern. But there's no predicting the different pieces it can smash into. And if you feel like your marriage is falling apart, you need to seek specific godly wisdom as to how to fit your marriage back together into the shape that Paul has for it, or what is 'fitting in the Lord.'

## 2. A Message for Husbands

Next there is a message for husbands in verse 19. 'Husbands, love your wives, and do not be harsh with them.'

Remember that Paul is addressing common failings that couples have within marriage. A woman may tend not to esteem her husband, but a man can tend to be angry, demean, and not adore his wife. It is important to see both these instructions—this one to husbands, as well as the previous to wives—in this context of typical temptations. So, Paul is not giving a total description of everything that could be said about being a husband. He is addressing tendencies to move in an unwise direction by nudging marriages back onto a path of a more Christlike relationship. Women can tend to undermine their

---

3    Leo Tolstoy, *Anna Karenina*, (Oxford: Oxford University Press, Reissue edition 2017), page 3.

husbands. They can tend to treat their husbands like their children; they can tend to mother their husbands, or even henpeck their husbands, and disrespect them. Men, on the other hand, can tend to not love their wives, not in authentically adoring ways. They can take them for granted. They can stop making much effort. They can even sneer at them and no longer cherish them.

Paul, then, like a surgeon cutting out a tumor rather than an author of a medical text book describing the whole human body, focuses on how husbands are to ensure that—above all else—they love their wives. It is fairly easy merely to say 'I love you.' It is harder to love your wife with humble service—with yard work, and dishes, and taking out the trash. Husbands: adore your wives not just with words but deeds. Maybe sometimes that seems more like an act of will than an overflow of sentiment. But Paul does not say 'you must have romantic feelings about your wife.' He says 'love your wives'; you can put love into practice even if you do not feel love. And often following from the practice afterwards will come the feeling.

A wife needs to know that she is the apple of her husband's eye. This means things like not ogling or staring at other women. How would that make your wife feel if you go out together on a date and you are staring at the waitress? Keep your eyes on your wife. Love *her*. Adore *her*. Be romantic towards *her*. Serve *her* practically in love.

Listen to the great Christian preacher Chrysostom describing the Christlike love a husband is to have for his wife:

> And even if it becomes necessary for you to give your life for her, yes, and even to endure and undergo suffering of any kind, do not refuse. Even though you undergo all this, you will

never have done anything equal to what Christ has done. You are sacrificing yourself for someone to whom you are already joined, but He offered Himself up for one who turned her back on Him and hated Him. In the same way, then, as He honored her by putting at His feet one who turned her back on Him, who hated, rejected, and disdained Him as He accomplished this not with threats, or violence, or terror, or anything else like that, but through His untiring love; so also you should behave toward your wife. Even if you see her belittling you, or despising and mocking you, still you will be able to subject her to yourself, through affection, kindness, and your great regard for her. There is no influence more powerful than the bond of love, especially for husband and wife. A servant can be taught submission through fear; but even he, if provoked too much, will soon seek his escape. But one's partner for life, the mother of one's children, the source of one's every joy, should never be fettered with fear and threats, but with love and patience.[4]

If you want to know what love means try reading again verses 12 to 14 of this very chapter 3 of the book of Colossians. Look at those virtues that we must 'put on' which are all held together by the harmony of love in the light of the call to love your wife:

- Compassion—being merciful not judgmental
- Kindness—being considerate and gentle
- Humility—secure in your own personality not prideful self-assertion
- Meekness—controlling your strength not lashing out
- Patience—perseverance and longsuffering not giving up
- Bearing with one another—carrying the burden of each other's weaknesses

---

4   A selection from *On Marriage and Family Life*, John Chrysostom, (St. Vladimir's Seminary Press), 1986.

- Forgiving one another—forgiving as you have been forgiven by Christ

That forgiving aspect of love is particularly crucial in marriage. I often think that the six most important words in married relationships are 'I am sorry' and 'I forgive you.' Some people become defensive when asked to forgive; they feel they are giving permission for bad behavior to continue. Consider, though, that forgiving someone does not mean their actions are acceptable. In fact, if their behavior were not wrong you would not need to forgive them. Nor does forgiving someone mean that you naively put yourself in the same position to be hurt again. Real restoration and complete reconciliation requires a renewed trust, and that comes from genuine repentance that leads to a changed life. On the other hand, you cannot hold off reconciliation until the other person is perfect! You will be waiting forever if that is your attitude. Certainly it is complicated, but so much of marriage renewal begins with the grace to accept that you are a sinner, that you married a sinner, that you are both on a journey of gradual sanctification. In the meantime you will need to forgive every day. And, if we are being frank, probably multiple times a day.

As Paul instructs husbands to love their wives, he also adds specifically 'and do not be harsh with them.' The word for harsh has the sense of 'embitter.' A wise husband avoids doing or saying what will cause a bitter root to grow up in his wife's heart. Don't speak angry, nasty and negative words. Don't shout. Don't storm around like a bull in a china shop. A man has physical and emotional power in a marriage. Speak *gently*. Speak *kindly*. Don't spend all your time complaining that the food is not the way you like it, or the décor is not how you want it, or that she has done this, that, or the other wrong. Don't stop her from being the person she is meant to be; seek her best, don't try to control her for your own selfish ambitions. In other words, don't be 'harsh' but instead 'love' her.

Think of the relationship with your wife as a bit like a bank account. Each time you say or do something harsh you are making a withdrawal. Each time you act in love you are making an investment. You want to be sure you don't dip into the red, embitter your wife, and go bankrupt. Maintain a healthy relational bank balance. To do that, you might even try writing a list at the end of each day of what you did for your wife. That way you will begin see whether you speak and act more lovingly or harshly. And you can adjust as needed.

## 3. A Message for Children

In verse 20 Paul has a message for children. 'Children, obey your parents in everything, for this pleases the Lord.' Paul is saying that 'children'—which we would define as those still living at home with their parents and under the age of eighteen—have a responsibility to obey their parents as this 'pleases the Lord.' What this means in practice is of course different for a three-year-old than for a fifteen-year-old. Wise parents gradually release the reins of obedience so that a child can learn bit by bit what it is to be an adult as they negotiate their teenage years. The developmental goal is that a child would in the end become a godly grown-up capable of independent living and flourishing.

Again, Paul is not here dealing with hard cases. Paul is not giving *carte blanche* to inadequate, inappropriate, much less evil, parenting. None of that 'pleases the Lord.' But if your parents are Christians and if they are acting in a way that is pleasing to the

Lord, are honorable and reasonably sensible, then as a child the responsibility is to obey.

What does that mean? It can be as simple as following specific instructions. For example, if you are asked to go to bed, go to bed the first time of asking, not the second or third or fourth! If you are asked to do some household chores, then do those chores without complaining. If your parents give you advice regarding your homework, listen and take it seriously.

It also means that you have a reason to do all of this that is bigger than merely pleasing mom or dad (who probably at least sometimes annoy you, after all). As a child, your motivation for obeying parents is not ultimately to please *them* but to please *the Lord*. A key expression of your spiritual vitality, your faith in Jesus, your worship of Jesus, your desire to please Jesus is, then, to obey your parents.

Children who grow up to do well in life tend to be those who have grasped opportunities when they were young to learn from wise adults. In most cases, your parents long for you to do well. They, more than anyone else in the entire world, normally have your interests at heart. And they want you to become the best possible version of yourself that you can be.

Some mothers and fathers do not parent well, and there are hard cases that go beyond Paul's simple, little description of how things should work in healthy Christian families. If you are being asked to do things that do not 'please the Lord,' then talk to a pastor, mentor or close friend, to help you figure out the right intervention strategy.

But generally speaking, your life will be best served, you will be more likely to thrive, if you learn to obey your parents, even when they say things that are difficult for you to hear. They want what is optimal for you and are trying to prepare you for a world outside where you will not always find loving, caring critiques, and there are people who are even out to hurt you and damage you. You need first to learn from your parents how to live in this sometimes brutal world outside the safety of home.

If there is a bone of contention between you and your parents, try to see if you can remove that conflict by simply obeying. Tidy your room, do your homework on time, study when you are asked to do so. You will be amazed how the spiritual atmosphere of a family can change, how the pleasure of Jesus can permeate the household, as a result of mere obedience to godly parents.

## 4. A Message for Fathers

In verse 21 Paul has a message for fathers. 'Fathers, do not provoke your children, lest they become discouraged.' Why does Paul only address fathers? It cannot be because he thinks mothers are unimportant; in the previous verse he says children are to obey *parents*, not just one parent. Paul is directing his teaching at a common problem. Fathers can tend to 'provoke' their children. They can be overly pushy. They can become harsh disciplinarians. 'You wait until your dad comes home.' They can demand too much, or even demean and belittle. There can be a tendency for men to work out their frustrations at home, adopt an angry lion sort of persona, and provoke their children to then be angry in return. If unaddressed, Paul is saying, this mode of fathering can lead to a child becoming 'discouraged.' The child feels dominated by their father, rather than being gently but firmly trained by their father how to be an adult on their own in the future.

Sometimes families with fathers like this can seem perfect while the children are still young. The father throws his weight around and makes sure that everyone looks good and acts right. What happens later, all too often, is that because the children are discouraged, one of two things occur: they either rebel or they become unable to take initiative as adults themselves. Some push back against their father's 'provoking' to rebel with a diametrically contrasting way of life. Others, though, stay infantilized; they have a near-constant dad voice in their head dominating their every move, unable to grow up to be who they were designed to be. They do not have the courage—they have been '*dis*couraged'—to take the frightening risk of following where God is leading to fulfill His purpose for their lives.

Now, if you have experienced something like this with your own father—maybe you had a bad father, or as is normal you had an imperfect father—look to God to '*en*courage' you. Yes, it is often a good idea seek an older, godly mentor. But you need more than a surrogate father figure (though a wise mentor avoids falling into that sort of Freudian trap). Really, you need to experience God as your Father. To trust Him. To love Him. To follow Him. And that will come as you listen to Him by His Spirit through His Word. Think of Samuel so long ago. Did he feel rejected by his own father? Perhaps he felt rejected by his mother too. At any rate, both parents were certainly, at least physically, if not emotionally, absent. There he was in the temple, with a potential surrogate father figure—the priest at the time. And yet what Samuel needed was to hear from God Himself. Open up the Bible, and say (as Samuel said), 'speak, Lord, for your servant hears' (1 Samuel 3:9). God's Word gives you strength, purpose and courage.

You who are Fathers are to avoid 'provoking' your children. You provoke your child when you lose your temper for no good reason. You provoke your child when you demand they behave in a way that is beyond their capabilities. You provoke your child when you insist they do what you want with their lives rather than what they are made for. The opposite of provoking your child comes from realizing that though they are your child, ultimately they are created by someone else. That means discovering how God has designed them. Observe carefully what they are good at, not what you wish they were good at. Make sure there is spiritual content in the home—Bible reading and prayer—so that they develop a prior relationship with their Heavenly Father. Be specific to communicate encouragement. Fathers, you have an extraordinary power to lift up your children. Tell them what they are good at, support and spur their development in their own areas of strength.

One illustration I sometimes use with fathers is of gardening. I'm not myself much of a gardener, but the image works for thinking through what it means to be a father. When you are given a child, it's a bit like being given a rose or a lily. You don't determine whether you have a rose or a lily; your child comes a certain way, with certain potentials and possibilities. Your job as a father is to nurture that. You need to observe who they are and what they are good at. Prune a little here, feed, water; prune some more, water some more. Protect from storms. But whatever you do, you're not going to change the rose to a lily or vice versa! What you can do is create a context in which your children have the opportunity to grow up to be the best possible version of who they were designed to be.

Fathers, identify where your children are gifted and tell them what you see. Put in the time to train them in what they are good at so that they can develop in those areas. Pray with your children that they would grow in their relationship with the Father God and become more like the person their Father wants them to be. Don't 'provoke' your children, or you will 'discourage' them. Instead, encourage them to follow God and serve Him in the special way He designed.

## 5. Employees

Having taught on holiness at home, Paul now comes to work. Verses 22-25 can be applied to how to be holy as an employee today.

Depending, though, on the translation you are using, these verses are more overtly specific instructions to those who are 'bondservants' or 'slaves.' Is it legitimate to apply this to the contemporary world of employment? Does the passage actually mean that the Bible supports slavery?

To understand how these verses can relate to working relationships in the modern world, it's important to have some historical background, as well as see this passage in the broader context of the Bible. In the seventeenth century, chattel slavery was tragically propagated across the Atlantic. The slave trade ripped human beings, made in the image of God, from their homes, brutally transported them to the other side of the world, and sold them into permanent slavery. It was a corrupt and evil system that treated a person as nothing more than a piece of property. In pre-Civil War America, slave masters would even use biblical texts to defend that institution of slavery.

However, Paul is not supporting chattel slavery, the transatlantic slave trade, or slavery as a whole. While some forms of ancient slavery were undeniably brutal and devilish, others were different from antebellum slavery. In ancient times, some slaves were doctors and teachers. Some even chose to remain slaves when they had the opportunity to become free. Slaves were sometimes prisoners of war. Slavery was also not always specifically racial in its institution—in fact, the word 'slavery' comes from the word for 'Slavic' because slaves were often white.

The word 'slaves,' here, then, is probably better translated—like some modern versions of the Bible—as 'bondservants.' Consider the ancient text of the *Didache* that reflects a somewhat similar attitude towards bondservants:

> Do not enjoin anything in your bitterness upon your bondman or maidservant, who hope in the same God, lest ever they shall fear not God who is over both; for he comes not to call according to the outward appearance, but to them whom the Spirit has prepared. And you bondmen shall be subject to your masters as to a type of God, in modesty and fear. You shall hate all hypocrisy and everything which is not pleasing to the Lord.[5]

A bondservant is not the same as a slave. A bondservant is bound to a master to exchange labor for room and board. In pre-modern Europe, bondservants were sometimes temporary—you might allow yourself to be bonded as a servant to pay down your debts, for instance, or for the cost of journeying to America. It is undoubtedly far too much of a stretch to say that employees today are the exact equivalent of 'bondservants,' but most employees are not 'masters' either, independently wealthy and free from the need to work for a living.

All that said, Paul is also not writing in favor of a somewhat milder, but still at best repressive and often abusively evil, form of slavery in ancient times. It is true Paul does not here tell slaves to revolt. But to what purpose would that instruction be if the means of change were not practically feasible? Where there

---

5    *The Didache*, Chapter 4.

were possibilities for ending slavery, Paul urged it. For instance, in the Book of Philemon, Paul encourages a master to accept his slave as now free ('no longer as a bondservant, but more than a bondservant, as a beloved brother', Philem. 16). And in 1 Corinthians, he tells slaves to gain their freedom if they possibly can ('if you can gain your freedom, avail yourself of the opportunity', 1 Cor. 7:21). Such biblical logic drove the anti-slavery movement to insist that social and political action be taken. It must motivate us to drive out modern forms of slavery today. Consider, the evangelical poet William Cowper's words:

> I had much rather be myself the slave
> And wear the bonds, than fasten them on him.
> We have no slaves at home - then why abroad?
> And they themselves, once ferried o'er the wave
> That parts us, are emancipate and loosed.
> Slaves cannot breathe in England; if their lungs
> Receive our air, that moment they are free,
> They touch our country and their shackles fall.
> That's noble, and bespeaks a nation proud
> And jealous of the blessing. Spread it then,
> And let it circulate through every vein
> Of all your empire; that where Britain's power
> Is felt, mankind may feel her mercy too.[6]

Or the prince of preachers', Charles Spurgeon's, even stronger words:

I do from my inmost soul detest slavery...and although I commune at the Lord's table with men of all creeds, yet with a slave-holder I have no fellowship of any sort or kind. Whenever one has called upon me, I have considered it my

---

6    From William Cowper, 'The Task', (1784), Book II.

duty to express my detestation of his wickedness, and I would
as soon think of receiving a murderer into my church...as a
man-stealer.[7]

The way this text, though, applies to many people today is to
being an employee (or what some euphemistically call being
a 'wage slave'). There are vital principles here about how to be
holy with relation to our employment. Paul says we are to 'work
not with eye-service as people-pleasers, but with sincerity of
heart, or with our whole heart, fearing the Lord.' That means
that ultimately you are working for Jesus. You don't just do 'eye-
service,' or only when your human boss is watching, because
really Jesus is your boss and He always sees what you are doing.
Fearing the Lord, you work hard and do your best at all times
with 'sincerity of heart.' That means things like not fudging your
expense account. Or, if your supervisor is out for the day, not
using his absence as a chance to neglect your job. Work just as
hard as if he were looking right over your shoulder. It means
not gossiping or undermining your boss, thinking he won't
know; God knows, He sees. But it also means you are free from
the approval of people. You are not a people-pleaser. You are
working for God.

Sometimes, of course, it can be hard at work when you
feel like you don't get the positive feedback that you think you
deserve, or that you are looking for from your boss or your
manager or supervisor. You think to yourself, 'Don't they care,
does no one notice all that I do?' The unvarnished truth may be
that your boss really doesn't notice what you do, but the bigger
truth is that God does. Your job is important to Jesus. You can

---

7    C. H. Spurgeon, cited from Arnold A. Dallimore, *Spurgeon: A Biography*,
     (Edinburgh, 1985).

be a lawyer or banker or street cleaner or student for Jesus just as much as a pastor for Jesus.

There is motivation in knowing that from the Lord you'll 'receive an inheritance as a reward.' We don't often think about rewards as Christians. It can perhaps seem legalistic, or anti-grace, but there is a reward for faithful Christian service. Look at it like this: when God rewards your work, He is rewarding Christ's work in you, and yet by His grace, you are rewarded for it. Amazing! It's a bit like if a starring football quarterback receives a trophy. There he is, he has his reward, but he immediately runs off and finds the coach who trained him ever since he was a little boy and says, 'This is for you.' And so, we give God the glory when He rewards us, for it is His work in us, and yet by His grace, He still rewards us. Think about that when you are struggling with your job. Think of the eternal reward for your faithful work for Jesus. He notices. He cares. And one day, you will be rewarded with joy in His presence forever.

But not only is there motivation from this reward, there is also a warning that acts as a comfort to those who are in a bad working situation. Paul says, 'For the wrongdoer will be paid back for the wrong he has done, and there is no partiality.' Ancient slavery could be relatively benign. There were doctors, physicians, and teachers who chose to remain as slaves as part of honored families. It could be like that. But it could also be horrendously, disgustingly, degradingly evil.

Work can be great—a good boss, good pay, well treated and appreciated for your work. And there can be vicious office politics, mobbing and bullying, reputations damaged through gossip and slander, not to mention all the sweatshops around the world today. Paul is saying that such wrongdoing is also noticed. We are living in a time when we anticipate Christ's second coming. And when King Jesus comes again, He will not only bring His reward with Him but also His judgment, where there will be, Paul says, 'no partiality.' God's judgment will not be based upon human prestige and power, but only on God's perfect justice.

Here are two future promises you can rely on of if you have worked in a situation where you are being abused, slandered, or mistreated. Not only will there be a 'reward' for your faithful service to Jesus, but the 'wrongdoer will be paid back' for any 'wrong' he or she has done when the second coming of Jesus occurs. Which, of course, also means we should all urgently turn from our own wrongdoing. Put your trust in Christ that He would raise you up and give you the spiritual power to follow Him.

## 6. Employers

As we look at these ways to be holy at home and work, we finally come to the bosses, or the employers. Colossians 4:1 says, 'Masters, treat your bondservants justly and fairly, knowing that you also have a Master in heaven.' We are applying this section to the contemporary working world (as explained above). If you have staff, or lead a group of people, then you have a responsibility to treat your team 'justly and fairly.' That means making sure that they are being paid a fair salary. Too often, bosses try to cut the bottom line by paying their staff as little as they can get away with while still keeping their staff. But Christian bosses have a responsibility to ensure their staff are being paid fairly.

How do you know what is fair? At College Church, we compare salaries in similar size ministries across the country to establish parameters for what we are paying our staff. We add in other factors like the cost of living, and consult with outside bodies to ensure we are doing what is fair, right and just. Then there are more subjective judgment calls, like how someone is performing in their job. There's probably no perfect way to know for sure whether someone is being paid fairly. The point is that we should be aiming to ensure that someone is paid fairly, rather than only paid what we can get away with paying them.

Treating your staff fairly goes beyond salary issues. It's the work environment, the kindness and respect with which employees are treated. And in a consumer economy, in a sense we all have staff. What about the pizza delivery person? Do we treat that person fairly as a person made in the image of God, and someone whom we can reach for Christ? What about the cleaner, or the person who bags your groceries at the grocery store? Or the person who cuts your hair? Do you just ignore them, or do you treat them as Christ would want you to? Do you care for them as you would like to be cared for by your Master in heaven?

In conclusion, let me give you four brief specific ideas as to how to put into practice being holy at home and at work.

1.   Ask a Question

First, if you are a wife or husband, father or child, would you take a step toward bringing your attitude and action into line with what Paul teaches here by asking the other person whether you are acting in this kind of way. Husbands, you could ask your wife, 'Am I being loving or being harsh?' Wives, you could ask your husband, 'Am I being respectful or undermining you?' Children, you could ask your parents, 'Am I being obedient or disobedient?'

2. Never Give Up

Second, though, perhaps you are in a difficult marital situation. Often over time, people reach a breaking point. They are not sure they can handle it anymore—the romantic expectations of near perfection clash with the real life experiences of imperfection, and they feel they cannot keep on going. Marriage is meant to be heavenly, but maybe you feel like you're in hell. Churchill once said, if you feel like you're going through hell, keep on going! The solution is not to look for an exit stage left. Breathe. Eat. Put one foot in front of the other. Trust that somehow in the muck, mess and mire, God still knows what He's doing. Don't give up. Don't throw in the towel. Make an appointment with a godly pastor. Begin the journey—it won't happen overnight, or in the next week or month; it might take years—of bringing life more in line with God's intention.

3. Pray Intentionally

Third, do not underestimate the power of committed praying. In many ways, the biggest influence you have over your spouse's behavior is through your prayers. Sometimes we might pray that the other person would change their attitude—and then discover that it is we who need to change, not them! Pray intentionally also if you are not yet married and long to be married. I don't mean saying a quick prayer one morning. I mean making a daily request, kneeling before God, and specifically asking Him to make you the sort of person you need to become to be married and to provide you with the person He wants you to marry. If you remain single, remember that Jesus was single, as was Paul who wrote these words. There is an honorable and significant role for single people in the church. Your worth is not based on your marital status—married or single.

4. Write a Reminder

Fourth, would you take a 3 x 5 card or a small piece of paper and write on it, 'Working with all my heart for the Lord, not for people.' Place it above your desk at home, your desk in the office or put it on your fridge in the kitchen. Find a way to keep that text in front of your eyes to remind you that you are working for the loving Lord whose eyes watch over you as you work.

As Paul emphasizes, it's all for Him and all by His power. That is the thread that runs throughout this passage. It's repeated actually seven times in these eight verses, *all for the Lord, as is fitting in the Lord, for the Master in heaven.* Over and over again, he's emphasizing that it is for the One who, we remember, will one day come again. For Him and in His power you can live in real gospel holiness both at home and at work.

## PRAYER

*Our Lord Jesus, we want to live for you. We pray, Lord, that our life and our words would speak of you, the Lord who has rescued us, in the way we live both at home and at work. In Jesus' name, Amen.*

# 6
# Relating to the Culture

[2] *Continue steadfastly in prayer, being watchful in it with thanksgiving.* [3] *At the same time, pray also for us, that God may open to us a door for the word, to declare the mystery of Christ, on account of which I am in prison—* [4] *that I may make it clear, which is how I ought to speak.* [5] *Walk in wisdom toward outsiders, making the best use of the time.* [6] *Let your speech always be gracious, seasoned with salt, so that you may know how you ought to answer each person.* (Col. 4:2-6)

Christianity has tended to lurch drunkenly between two extremes when it comes to relating to the culture. On the one hand, it has tried so hard to engage with the culture around that it has become in many ways indistinguishable from those it is trying to reach. To illustrate the problem with this approach, I imagine what a fish would say if it was asked how it would like to be fished. 'More bait, less hook, please,' is how I would expect

101

a fish might reply. Similarly, some Christian movements have not only dumbed down practical Christianity to the standards of the 'fish' they have tried to reach, they have almost become fish themselves. But, on the other hand, there are Christian movements that have reacted so strongly against 'compromise' that they move a thousand miles away from the fish. Their fishing boat is not even in the water. Often, a call to 'holiness' is paralleled with an ineffective and uncreative evangelistic approach. Neo-monastic movements that urge people 'away from the world' can create barriers to connecting with people 'in the world.' To reach people, the people need to be within reach.

What is the right approach? It is fascinating that as Paul encourages the Colossians towards holiness, he is also urging them to engage with 'outsiders.' No walking away from non-Christians for Paul. No separation and lack of engagement with Paul. But, as we have already seen, no compromise morally either. How can we depict his approach?

The problem is we tend to think in terms of sales when it comes to evangelism. We market the gospel. We sell the gospel. But we don't need more salesmen; what we need is more free samples. We need more Christlikeness. And of course Christ came to seek and save that which is lost—and so should we who follow Christ. Think of outreach not as sales or marketing, but as being an ambassador. And think of the church not as a business with a product to push on its customers, but as an embassy. The embassy will be more effective at commending the mother country to the outsiders around only if the embassy is like the best possible version of the country from which it is sent.

Here in these verses, then, Paul gives us three ways to relate, as holy Christ-followers, 'in the world but not of the world,' to those who are not yet Christians.

## *Pray Passionately*

The first way is to pray. Verse 2 says, 'Continue steadfastly in prayer, being watchful in it with thanksgiving.' The phrase 'continue steadfastly' does not intend a begrudging or boring attendance at a staid, old-fashioned, sleep-inducing, prayer meeting. It means to be devoted to, committed to, enthusiastic and eager about, passionate prayer.

For effective outreach is only the tip of the iceberg. Underneath is prayer. One revival I was a part of had prayer as its hidden power. In a single week we saw a hundred students at a small school become Christians. Afterwards I discovered that a group of committed Christian teachers had gathered every Saturday morning for ten years to pray for revival.

In 1857 businessmen began a weekly prayer meeting in New York City. As people with a demanding schedule, they determined it was to last for just one hour starting at 12 noon. At first only six people came. But soon enough it was packed. Then they had to meet every day to accommodate all the people who wanted to attend. Then in several different locations. It ended up spreading across the country, with business people in the thousands meeting to pray for revival. From such persistence in prayer was born a nationwide spiritual awakening.

Paul says we are to 'continue steadfastly in prayer.' One of the great secrets of prayer is simply not to give up. Jesus told the story of the widow who needed justice against her enemy. She went to an unjust judge. The unjust judge had no desire to give her justice. But the widow kept on asking and asking and asking.

Eventually the judge gave her justice because that was the only way to get her to leave him alone! By contrast, Jesus says, how much more will God give justice to His children who constantly cry out to Him day and night. Jesus told this story to teach His disciples that we should always pray and not give up. That is, as Paul puts it here, we should continue steadfastly in prayer.

E.M. Bounds in his classic book *Power Through Prayer* tells the story of one great Christian leader who 'wore the hard-wood boards into grooves where his knees pressed so often and so long.' A biographer of this great Christian leader said of him, 'To his ardent and persevering prayers must no doubt be ascribed in a great measure his distinguished and almost uninterrupted success.'[1]

Perhaps you have a friend who is not yet a Christian. Perhaps you have a neighbor or a family member who is not yet a Christian. Perhaps you see spiritual drift in your church, city, or country. Pray. Don't give up. Pray perseveringly, continually, steadfastly, passionately.

How? Prayer is a conversation between you and God and like all conversations it has its own personal rhythm. But that said, the organic and spontaneous nature of talking with God is greatly aided by being deliberate. For instance, write a prayer list of people and churches to pray for. Or try creating a calendar entry on your phone as a way of specifically scheduling time for praying like you would schedule any other appointment. If your calendar is shared with others, you could be creative in how you describe the calendar entry; call it a meeting with your Boss! Pray also as you go through the day. Learn the habit of praying

---

1    E.M. Bounds, *Power Through Prayer*, (CreateSpace, 2011), page 31.

before you answer a phone call, before you write an email, as you are talking with a non-Christian about Jesus.

I know someone who prayed steadfastly for their large wider family, and over the years all but one of them came to faith in Christ. The great ancient Christian leader Augustine was converted through the faithful prayers over many years of his mother Monica. Pray; then, pray; then, pray some more! Do not give up.

And, says Paul, be 'watchful.' Paul is probably referring to Jesus' teaching about prayer that we are not just to pray but to *watch and* pray. When we pray we are to have a wide-awake, watchful consciousness of the shortness of time because we know that at any moment Jesus could return. Some people tend to think of prayer as merely calming and gentle. Instead, prayer is to be urgent and passionate because it is 'watchful.' Pray with committed devotion, for any moment time could run out and Jesus could return. When we pray we are to be alert knowing Jesus is coming back. Not like the wedding guests who fell asleep waiting for the bridegroom to arrive; no, watchful, awake, attentive, active, engaged. The prayerful somnolence of a monotone ritual prayer is not 'steadfastly praying being watchful.' As the famed evangelist D.L. Moody would say, 'Some men's prayers should be cut short at either end and set on fire in the middle'![2]

We are to be watchful. Jesus is coming back. We have urgent work to do including the work of prayer. Wake up; pray; He will come at an hour you do not expect. Pray with your eyes on Jesus' return. The great Christian leader John Wesley said that

---

2    Or as one ancient text put it, 'Watch for your life's sake' (*Didache*, chapter 16).

he 'valued all things only by the price they shall gain in eternity.' Similarly, prayer is fueled by an eyes-wide-open scanning for Jesus' immediate return and the ushering in of the eternal age to come.

And also, Paul says, pray with 'thanksgiving.' How often do we miss out on joy because we neglect giving thanks. How often are we sad when we could celebrate because we do not give thanks. How often are our prayers burdened by grumbles when they are meant to soar to heaven with thanksgiving! Horizontal moaning prayer about each other is prevented by vertical thanksgiving to God. The dead weight of prayer as a horizontal litany of complaints is lifted up to the vertical with thanksgiving to God.

If you haven't already, how about identifying a specific daily time to pray? If you already have a time set aside to pray, could you find an extra five minutes to ensure you also thank God for all He has done in your life? With thanksgiving lifting you, commit to steadfast, persistent, praying for those who do not yet know Christ, watchful for when Christ comes back.

## Pray for Preachers

The second way to relate to those who do not yet believe in Christ is to pray for those who preach Christ. In verses 3 and 4 Paul says, 'At the same time, pray also for us, that God may open to us a door for the word, to declare the mystery of Christ, on account of which I am in prison— that I may make it clear, which is how I ought to speak.' Not only are we to pray for those who do not yet know Jesus, we are also to pray for those who preach Jesus.

Sometimes pastors are wary of asking people to pray for them for fear that it will come across as self-serving. Do not other people need prayer more? But Paul had no qualms about asking for prayer. Here, and in many other places in the New Testament, he asks God's people directly to pray for him:

- 'I appeal to you... to strive together with me in your prayers to God on my behalf' (Rom. 15:30)
- 'You must also help us by prayer' (2 Cor. 1:11)
- '[Pray] also for me, that words may be given to me in opening my mouth boldly to proclaim the mystery of the gospel' (Eph. 6:19)
- 'For I know that through your prayers and the help of the Spirit of Jesus Christ this will turn out for my deliverance' (Phil. 1:19)
- 'Brothers, pray for us' (1 Thess. 5:25)
- 'Finally, brothers, pray for us that the word of the Lord may speed ahead and be honored' (2 Thess. 3:1)

God's people are to pray for God's leaders. If private prayer is the great secret to public success, then the prayers of the church for their pastor are the great secret to a pastor's effectiveness. There is certainly much to pray for. Listen to how Methodist bishop Thomas Coke put it:

'To be good preachers of Jesus Christ, and of him crucified, we must ourselves be fastened to the cross of Jesus Christ: to inspire a taste of God, and the things of heaven, we must feel them ourselves: to touch the hearts of the people, our own hearts must be touched with the living coal.'[3]

The pressures that pastors are under these days is ever increasing. They are rarely paid enough to not be tempted to worry about their finances. They are called to only please one Master in

---

3    Thomas Coke, *The Duties of a Minister of the Gospel*, (1810; The Master Christian Library), page 32.

heaven and yet often their practical livelihood is in the hands of the opinion of the masses on earth. No one would watch an episode of the long-running hospital TV show *E.R.* and then tell their surgeon how to do surgery, but many a church attender believes that having gone to church he knows full well how best to preach in church.

The renowned pastor Jonathan Edwards had enemies. They not only resisted the revival he led, pushed for his removal from his pulpit, but even ending up following him to continue their attacks when he went to serve a missionary outpost. They spread gossip and lies about him to his new employers, hoping to have him fired not just once but twice. Far from being easier today, the role of a pastor is harder. The spiritual opposition that goes with the territory of being a preacher is now amplified further by the power of social media, which threatens all public figures with an ever-present potential for reputational ruin. What is more, we seem today to be ever on the edge of anger with our leaders and being outraged by those who say anything of which we disapprove—and a large part of a preacher's job is to say what we need to hear even if it isn't what we want to hear. On top of this is the gradual drip feed devaluation of respect for the role of pastors in secular society today.

'*Pray also for us*,' a pastor and preacher—even an apostle— says. The damage that can be afflicted on the church at large through attacks on its leaders is immense: 'strike the shepherd and the sheep will scatter.' And conversely the wounds of a faithful pastor are many as he gives his life to protect the flock, whether or not he is physically in prison.

But note what it is that Paul wants them to pray for: 'That God may open to us a door for the word, to declare the mystery of Christ, on account of which I am in prison.' What a man was Paul! Here he is in prison, yet his prayer is for the progress of the gospel. He wants God to open a door for the Word or the mystery of Christ, which is Paul's shorthand for the now-revealed good news about Jesus. So Paul is asking them to pray not specifically for the doors of his *prison cell* to be opened, but for the doors of *people's hearts* to be opened. Paul above all wanted to proclaim Christ effectively.

I ask you to pray that God would grant me an open door for the preaching of the gospel. And to pray the same for any gospel preacher that you know. That many people would be open to hear the gospel. That God would grant open doors of opportunity for the good news of Jesus that we preach to make progress everywhere.

To that end Paul asks them to pray, 'that I may make it clear, which is how I ought to speak.' To make clear means to 'make manifest or visible what has been hidden,' to 'expose' something, or make 'plain.' The 'it' which Paul wants to make clear is the mystery of Christ. That mystery was revealed in God coming as a baby in a manger, Christ dying for our sins on the cross, rising again from the dead.

This is the mystery, or good news, that Paul wants them to pray that he would make clear, make manifest, visible, plain, expose or exposit. This is why we are to teach the Bible, not just from the pulpit but in children's ministries and to teenagers and seniors too. This is why the gospel or good news is to be at the center of everything we do. We are to make clear the gospel from the Bible. The goal is not to give life coach lessons. The goal is to make plain the good news of Jesus.

Sometimes the good news is clear but hearts are shut; other times hearts are open but the good news is confused. For there to be effective outreach to those who do not yet know Christ we need *both* clear good news *and* open hearts.

Would you make a resolution to pray for all your pastors that God would grant an open door for their ministries and that they would make clear the good news of Christ? How about setting aside a moment today to pray for this week's church services that God would grant an open door in many people's hearts for the gospel and that the gospel would be clear?

## *Live Wisely*

The third way to relate to those who are not yet Christians is to adopt a wise way of life or, as Paul calls it, to 'walk in wisdom.' In verses 5 and 6 Paul says, 'Walk in wisdom toward outsiders, making the best use of the time. Let your speech always be gracious, seasoned with salt, so that you may know how you ought to answer each person.'

When Paul says we are to walk in 'wisdom,' though, he is not just telling the Colossians to live sensibly or prudently. He is referring to specific teaching about wisdom already given in the letter. In chapter two, Paul had told them that in Christ are hidden 'all the treasures of wisdom and knowledge' (Col. 2:3). He taught them this so that they would not be led astray by false teachers: 'I say this so that no one may delude you with plausible arguments' (Col. 2:4). Paul was making the case that because all the wisdom they need is in Christ, therefore there was no need to listen to the false teachers. Don't listen to those who claim to have a new or better wisdom. In Jesus you already have all wisdom and knowledge! Don't let the false teachers 'delude' you with their apparently sophisticated, or wise, religious rules and rituals. Stick to Christ. He has all the wisdom there is.

So to 'walk in wisdom' toward 'outsiders' is not simply being prudent, careful, or sensible in how we interact with non-Christians. Nor is it merely learning 'wise' techniques of evangelism, much less a clever proselytizing formula. No, to 'walk in wisdom' is to develop a revitalized relationship with Christ so that you walk as He did—you follow Jesus' way of life and therefore Jesus' way of reaching 'outsiders.'

Read how Jesus reached the woman at the well. Study how He spoke to Nicodemus. Observe the way He reached Zacchaeus. Marvel at His interaction with the Pharisees and Scribes. To walk in wisdom towards outsiders is to emulate that kind of pattern of life: loving, merciful, strong, kind, gracious, firm, a life lived to rescue others. Jesus spent time with those He wished to reach. He ate with them. He talked with them. He challenged them. He knew them. He asked them questions. He told them stories. He did not treat everyone the same. It was the same message, but not the same people. Pharisees rebuked, sinners loved, disciples trained.

The book of Proverbs says 'he who wins souls is wise' (Prov. 11:30, NKJV). A wise Christian does not quote verses at random around the dinner table, hitting his non-Christian family members over the head with the Bible. She does not dump theological truth on her friends in a discussion thread online, burying them underneath an avalanche of spiritual jargon.

Wise Christians are not on a legalistic hit-and-run job, guilt-tripping Twitter followers to leave people bleeding from religious guilt. A wise Christian in love listens carefully to the hurting without condemnation. And in the fear of God speaks the truth in love to the misguided. It is wisdom to know not only what you should say but how you should say it and when.

A wise Christian knows that they cannot convert someone by their own power. I cannot manipulate you or emotionally trick you to follow Christ. You must be raised with Christ.

To walk in wisdom, Paul says, requires 'making the best use of the time.' The word that is translated as 'making the best use of' means to redeem or buy back, to take full advantage of or seize a buying opportunity. The word occurs on four occasions in the New Testament. Twice in the book of Galatians describing how Christ has redeemed us, or bought us back, from legalistic religious slavery (Gal. 3:13, 4:5). And then in Ephesians (Eph. 5:16) and here in Colossians talking about making the best use of time once we are Christians. The inner gospel logic of these uses of this word 'redeem' seems to be that as we have been redeemed by Christ, now we are to redeem the time He has given us. We have been set free, now we are to live as free people. We have been bought back from slavery, now we have the opportunity to make the most of the time. Seize the opportunity!

Management legend Peter Drucker is reported to have emphasized, 'Until we can manage time, we can manage nothing else.' But if you are redeemed by Christ you can redeem, or make the best use of, time even on an eternal timescale! Christian, you can give your life for something that lasts forever. Paul wants you to redeem your time not just so that you can be more productive in an economic sense but in an eternal sense. He wants you to redeem your time so you can invest in people. He wants you to redeem the time for eternity by bringing non-Christians to Christ. Redeem your time by telling others about Christ. That way you will invest your life in what lasts forever. Would you review your calendar, your to-do list, to see how much of your time is redeemed—that is, how much is used for telling people about Jesus? Would you pray for opportunities to tell people about Jesus and then make the most of those opportunities when they come? Would you redeem your time by sending out emails or texts to your friends asking them to come with you to church?

So we are to live wisely as followers of Christ, making the best use of our time, and also our speech is to be 'gracious.' Verse 6, 'Let your speech always be gracious, seasoned with salt, so that you may know how you ought to answer each person.'

Gracious speech is not merely saying nice things; it means speaking in a way that reflects the grace of God. If someone is living in a way that you do not approve, not harshly condemning them but remembering that you too need the grace of God. If someone does something wrong, remembering that you too are a wrongdoer who daily depends on the grace of God. When you have the opportunity, articulating the message of God's grace, the good news of Jesus.

But not only is our speech to be gracious, it is also to be 'seasoned with salt.' In the ancient world salt had two purposes. There were then no refrigerators, so salt was a preservative to keep food edible longer. And salt of course also made food taste better. So to season your speech with salt preserves the good in society by promoting what is right, and arouses curiosity in Christ by stimulating the mental taste buds. Sometimes that means finding a way to break the stereotypes. 'Christians are all so judgmental,' a family member says to you. You reply, 'well isn't it judgmental to say that all Christians are judgmental?' Sometimes it means dropping comments like salted peanuts to generate thirst or interest. 'Did you know that there are about 2.2 billion Christians today? That's a third of the population of the world. By far the largest religion. Maybe it's worth taking a look at the claims of Christ.'

So with wisdom, making the best use of the time, speech that is gracious and seasoned with salt, we will know how we 'ought to answer each person.' For instance, if someone asks you a question that you do not know the answer to, you could say, 'Thanks. That's a good question. I'm not sure of the answer, can I think about it and get back to you in a day or two?' Then you could talk to a pastor and get back to the person with a satisfying answer. Or if someone says to you, 'Yes of course I'm a Christian, and yes I know the Bible says I shouldn't do that, but I'm going to do it anyway because I want to and God will forgive me.' You could say something like, 'Forgiveness has a condition: repentance. Jesus says those who love me will obey my commandments.' Or if someone says to you 'I feel I am wasting my life and I don't know what to do.' You could say something like, 'the good news is that Jesus came to redeem us so that we could redeem the time to make the most of our lives and do something that will have value forever. Why not give your life to Jesus? Why not join me in inviting other people to come to church?'

So be holy in relation to those who are not yet Christians, pray passionately, pray for preachers, and live—including speaking—wisely.

## Three Ways to Put it into Practice

In conclusion, here are three brief ways to put this into practice. The first I have already alluded to. Invite people to come with you to a gospel-preaching church. Most people need to be asked. Would you extend an invitation to someone you know to come to church with you to hear the gospel preached? Second, pray for God to open hearts. Would you pray specifically for God to open hearts to the message of the gospel? Third, perhaps you are someone who is not yet a Christian. I hope you are encouraged to hear Christians are to use no manipulation, or underhand sales techniques. Would you ask God to raise you up with Christ? I pray God would open your heart to receive Christ. I pray that you would receive the mystery of Christ which is now made manifest: God sent His Son as a baby to live and die that whoever believes would be raised with Christ.

## PRAYER

*Our Lord God, we do pray. We pray, Lord, for those who don't yet know you, that you would break their chains and raise them up. We pray, Lord, for the preaching of your word, the gospel, Lord, that there would be open doors, open hearts and a clear message. O Lord, we pray for our own daily lifestyle, particularly around those who do not know you. We have opportunities to say something about you, and at times we find it difficult to know what to say. We pray you would give us wisdom and that our conversation would always be gracious, filled with the grace that you have given us and reflecting that grace and speaking of that grace and also seasoned with salt. Give us the right things to say at the right time. So, we bow before you and come and worship in the name of Jesus. Amen.*

# 7

# *A Christian Orange*

*A Clockwork Orange* is a famous dystopian—and rather violent—look at the future. In the novel, ethical behavior has become so bad that the State has decided that drastic measures must be taken. The recalcitrant youths are sent through a demeaning system of reeducation that is intended to rewire their brains and make them docile.[1]

More recently, the book *The Handmaid's Tale* reworks the dystopian future trope to speculate that it is a religious group that is dominating us to make us behave.[2] Our nightmares betray us: are we more scared of a totalitarian secular regime enforcing conformity, or of a religious 'Taliban'? George Orwell's *Nineteen Eighty-Four*, with its vision of Big Brother watching over us,[3]

1   Anthony Burgess, *A Clockwork Orange* (Heinemann, 1962).

2   Margaret Atwood, *The Handmaid's Tale* (McClelland & Stewart, 1985).

3   George Orwell, *Nineteen Eighty-Four* (Secker & Warburg, 1949).

vies for prescience with Aldous Huxley's *Brave New World*, with its vision of sexual chaos.[4]

Strange to say, churches—and Christian leaders—can fall into some of these traps. What to do with people (ourselves included) who do not live up to the standards that Christ inspires? How do we dig out—root as well as branch—the evil? Is an *Inquisition* required? A witch trial? Monasteries? Puritanical dress codes?

Such questions are far from theoretical when we see looting in our streets, machine guns killing our children, or marriages falling apart. You can begin to understand why, in a moment of weakness, someone might decide that the only practical course of action is some sort of 'clockwork orange.'

But it is not the Christian way. When Christ calls us to follow Him, He bids us come and die (yes) but also to come back to life. We, with trust in Christ, have been raised with Him! Our task is not to invent a new set of rules, or disciplines, that will enforce behavior. Our task is not to set our alarm clock ever earlier in order to ensure that we look like Christians, even though we are not really. Our task is to be (increasingly) what and who we are. We are beloved. We are graced. We are His; in Him we live.

The lie is that as we give our lives to Christ we will become less truly ourselves. But the reverse is true: by giving up the false, and fake, self we will gradually—bit by bit—become more truly ourselves. We are made for Him. Like a fish is made for water, we are made to swim in His beauty. A fish is not more free out of water. It is free when it is set free to swim in its element. And as we dive into the love of Christ more deeply and truly, as we embrace the work of the Spirit of Christ in our lives, we become

---

4    Aldous Huxley, *Brave New World* (Chatto & Windus, 1932).

more who we were made to be. Not, if you like, a 'clockwork' orange—enforced against our will to conform. But instead, the person Christ has designed.

Christian: be who you are.

# Appendix A:
## A Brief History of Holiness

Ideas are like genes: you inherit more than you sometimes realize. When it comes to an idea like 'holiness,' we are using a word that has its own embodied history within it. We may not be consciously aware of that history, but it impacts the kind of conversation we have. For one person the word 'holiness' relates to the holiness movement of the early twentieth century, evangelical Protestantism. For another person, the word 'holiness' is more about a Roman Catholic view of the spiritual disciplines. For yet another, the word 'holiness' brings with it Eastern Orthodox ideas of being 'partakers of the divine nature.' For yet another individual, the word 'holiness' just feels heavy— perhaps this is the most common feeling that people have when they hear the word—because it somehow conjures up images of weighty morality. I remember when I was writing on morality for my atheistic Cambridge professor, I used the phrase 'the weight of morality.' He wanted to analyze why—knowing I was a Christian—I was still using that image for morality. Was it a weight to me personally? Did I see morality as a burden? Of course, he was hoping that I would begin to be enlightened, and learn to see the world through a more atheistic lens. But then there are the other religious views of holiness. For many millions of people today, holiness means the pillars of Islam. For still others, it somehow relates to the noble path of the Buddha.

Still more complicatedly, Western intellectual history since the secularizing impact of the Enlightenment has been marked by lengthy attempts to demonstrate the ethical possibilities of becoming 'holy' without God. To this extent, I still tend to think it is not really possible to understand where we are as a society without reading Immanuel Kant's *A Critique of Pure Reason*, and at least partly understanding it. To grasp it you have to grasp whom he is talking to: all this conversation going back not just to Augustine with his famous *Confessions* but, of course, to the Ancients, also Aristotle, Plato and Socrates, to the debates between the Stoics and the Epicureans, on into the Middle Ages, and then to the doubts and denials of Rousseau, D'Alembert and Giambattista Vico and eventually David Hume.

Obviously, I cannot survey all this in a couple of paragraphs or so, but I do think it is important that the reader knows that I know—and even more important, can give some guidance as to how to navigate. Are there patterns regarding holiness that can be discerned, that then impact the way we think about 'holiness' today? I think the answer to that is certainly 'yes' and I will outline it now (as I say) briefly.

To begin with, the key issue is the doctrine of depravity. What an old-fashioned word! But if we do not think we have fallen so far, we will not think we need such a radical remedy.

The central problem of all incorrect views of holiness is to misdiagnose the problem. Essentially, we tend to say that we are not so sick and therefore we do not need such radical surgery. This is why 'Christian' (I put it in quotes to indicate that it has little to do with what Christ taught), as well as non-Christian, religions are alike in their view of holiness. They are saying that the answer is to adopt certain techniques—the language differs as to how these techniques are described, but the remedy is always to adopt certain techniques. Here are the habits you need to inculcate. Here are the disciplines you need to adopt. Here are the rules to follow. Here is the noble path. Here is the regimen.

But if we actually believe—what the Bible teaches—which is that we are dead in sin, we would not be offering people little rules to help. Someone who is dead will not be made alive by being given a pamphlet on how to run better, or sit up, or walk. What they need is a resurrection.

So the starting issue is always to clarify the real nature of the problem. We are dead. Let us start there. We need a resurrection. Or (as Jesus put it) to be born again. Without clarity as to the problem, we will never have clarity as to the solution.

But then the second greatest issue that is a common pattern is the need to understand who Christians actually are. If we do not grasp what we are as Christians, we will not have a real understanding of how we can (as it were) become more Christian. I find that Christians swing between being naïve or depressive in this regard. Rarely are we realistic. This too is at least partly because of the history around the use of the word holiness, and teaching related to it. One common approach has been to build—often physical but sometimes social—walls to keep 'the bad guys out'. But this is to misunderstand who we are as Christians. We cannot keep the bad stuff out. We have the bad stuff within us. Yes, a Christian is 'raised with Christ'. But also, yes, a Christian still has a fight on their hands. We have the old nature with us. Sin must be put to death, sometimes on a daily basis. It is no good, as down through church history so many people have attempted, to try to become more holy by simply gathering with other Christians in some sort of enclosed ghetto. We bring the sin with us. What we need is a far more radical remedy. I talk about this in the book at some length: putting sin to death.

That said, there is another side to this which also has been frequently underemphasized: who we are in Christ. In this regard, I always find that it is important to emphasize to people that when someone really becomes holy they become more normal. Being holy is not being weird. It's being more like you were made to be. It's being more like you, as you are in Christ. Jesus was not weird. Was there ever anyone more human? Of course not, for He was (is) the ideal man. So there is this issue of identity which shapes this whole book: being who we are in Christ.

In essence, then, I would say that in a (necessarily) brief survey of history as it relates to holiness, the basic pattern is a lack of clarity as to who we are. Who we are when we are not Christians, and who we are when we are Christians. And it is this emphasis which shapes the New Testament teaching too: become who you are in Christ. The best teachers on holiness throughout church history have emphasized this, and rather than repeat their words here again I point the reader to the quotations from them that are littered throughout the book.

# Appendix B:
## Spiritual Warfare and Holiness

This, I suspect, is the most difficult few paragraphs I will ever write. When C.S. Lewis talked about how he wrote of the work of the devil in his famous *Screwtape Letters* he suggested it was not that hard once you got the hang of it—though he didn't seem to think it was a particularly pleasant, much less danger-free, exercise. *Au contraire*, I think that trying to put into words, especially in just a few words, the spiritual dynamic related to holiness—without leading us down rabbit trails or up proverbial creeks without a paddle—is, well, difficult.

It may surprise some of you to know that a few years ago I began to explore the literature around demonic possession (as it is usually, if not always accurately, called). There is actually a fair amount written on it, though I will not give you any tips as to where to find it as I cannot say I found the experience particularly edifying. The reason I started to read around about this tricky topic is because, as a pastor, one does sometimes come across odd things. In my ecclesial background, there are not many choices open to you when you start to have questions about this particular area of human experience. There is the literature and practice of Pentecostal and Charismatic deliverance ministries. There is the literature and practice of Roman Catholic (and I assume also Orthodox) exorcisms. Then there are the secular theories about the psychology of such experiences.

But what does the Bible say about it? What do you do when—as I recently encountered—you come across a situation when both you and the medical professional with whom you are working can only say to one another 'that seems potentially demonic'?

Of course, the easy (and correct) answer is 'well, of course it's demonic.' The devil wears Prada...he does not come wearing a tail and horns, he shows up in a BMW with a nice, perfect, lifestyle and plenty of pearly white teeth. Biblically, we are either in Christ, or we are under the power of the evil one.

Nonetheless, there are experiences in this regard that do not sit neatly within easy categories. And, it seems to me, it would be remiss of me not to acknowledge the effect they can have in trying to help people cast off burdens and grow in Christlikeness. As the renowned Swedish theologian and novelist Bo Giertz boldly wrote, 'he still has his cloven hoof within the door of our hearts.'[1] Evil is real. Even secular histories acknowledge as much, like the remarkable Yale University Press published history of the occult in the Third Reich.[2] Or As Dietrich Bonhoeffer said

---

1   Bo Giertz, *The Hammer of God*, (Augsburg, 2005), page 99.
2   Eric Kurlander, *Hitler's Monsters: A Supernatural History of the Third Reich,* (Yale University Press, 2018).

before he died, 'One is distressed by the failure of reasonable people to perceive either the depths of evil or the depths of the holy.'[3]

For want of any more full treatise, then, I pass along these few thoughts that may help fellow warriors. First of all, be diligent in both being filled with the Spirit and wearing the armor of God. I won't go into detail here about how to do either of those two things, except to say that if you wish to fight a spiritual battle you had better be in tip-top spiritual shape and have a set of gospel-strengthened convictions that can give you protection. Second, pray. I know, I know, obvious, right? But why do we think Paul emphasizes, in the context of talking about spiritual warfare, that we are to pray in the Spirit. I think our teaching on prayer is too *technical.* It's too *methodological.* Prayer is a fight; it's not like breathing, it's like waging war. Third, take the devil seriously but not too seriously. Yes he prowls around like a roaring lion looking to devour someone, but if you resist him he'll flee from you. His great trick is to get you to fear him. Stand up to him. You're a Christian, right? Don't give the devil the time of day. Focus on Jesus—at His name demons run away. I've always loved Luther on spiritual warfare: if all else fails, even the Word, try laughter. The devil is a proud devil and he can't stand being laughed at. He is defeated. Alleluia.

---

3    Banner of Truth magazine, May 2018, page 2.

# Appendix C:
## Holiness and Mental Health

How our psychology impacts our habits, our behavior, our performance, our feelings, and therefore our practical holiness is surprisingly seldom considered in some Christian circles. Or maybe not surprisingly: it is such a vast area of complexity, and controversy, that it is easier or simpler to leave the conversation to the 'professionals' and let the church focus on 'spiritual' matters. For many reasons this is a mistake. To begin with, as social and religious commentators frequently acknowledge, we live in a therapeutic age.[1] We are the children of not just Freud and Jung but of countless pop-psychology and internet therapies. Americans especially; the British are still more likely to talk to a friend about their problems than to a counselor. Or at least they were when I was growing up there; perhaps it has changed. At

---

1    E.g. Charles Taylor, *Sources of the Self*, (Harvard, 1992); Carl R. Trueman, *The Rise and Triumph of the Modern Self*, (Crossway, 2020).

any rate, for the church to ignore the impact of psychology on how we think about motivation and impulses and morality is a mistake of gargantuan proportions. I remember one mature Christian leader who was sharing with me some of the personal struggles he had faced over many years. When he eventually went to see a psychologist he was flummoxed to find that the advice given him in that context 'worked' when more mundane instructions had failed. Until, he said, he realized that much of the advice given him by the counselor mirrored what he could have seen in the Bible if he had had eyes to see.[2]

What makes this all the more difficult is that within the relatively small world of Christian ministry, there is something of a pitched battle between different definitions and descriptions of what is healthy psychology and counseling and what is not. Broadly speaking, there are those who take an integrative approach—utilizing the Egypt's gold of secular counseling insights combined with Biblical tools—and there are those who reject that sort of integration. Sometimes the difference is determined by the terminology of either being a 'Christian counselor' (and therefore meaning that you take an integrative approach) or a 'Biblical counselor' (meaning that you purport to only take instructions from the shape of the teaching of the Bible and of the gospel).

Some of this is made worse by the lack of familiarity with the long heritage of Christian teaching related to what we would

---

2   I have found that talking about 'mental health' tends to expose you to accusations of lack of empathy. I assume that most readers will think that I have had little personal experience of challenges with mental health. But that is not the case. I choose to keep those challenges private, though they are not secret. All I can say is that for most of my life achieving what is today called mental health has been a blood-soaked fight.

call mental health. People seem to assume that psychology was discovered by Freud—rather than the psychological techniques unearthed in those days as signs that people were not looking to pastors or the church for help in these areas when previously they had done so. If you doubt me in this regard, think of the massive tome written by Richard Baxter called *A Christian Directory.*[3] Page after page, Baxter shows masterful insight as to how to help people with their pains. Or look at just this one instance from Owen on the importance of distinguishing between the spiritual and the temperamental or mental:

> Learn to distinguish the effect of natural distempers from spiritual diseases. Some have sad, dark, and tenacious thoughts fixed on their minds from their natural distempers. These will not be cured by reasonings, nor utterly quelled by faith. Our design must be, to abate their efficacy and consequents by considering their occasions. And if men cannot do this in themselves, it is highly incumbent on those who make application of relief unto them to be careful to discern what is from such principles, whereof they are not to be expected a speedy cure.[4]

My task, though, in this appendix is more modest than attempting to defuse this bomb of controversy, much less put a stick in the hornet's nest and stir up trouble. I want to share with you some of my pastoral insights, hard-won from the coalface of helping people overcome various difficulties in their lives. First of all, I think many pastors are woefully out of date with their understanding of psychology. To remedy this, you need not

---

3    Richard Baxter, *A Christian Directory,* (1673; Soli Deo Gloria, 1996).

4    John Owen, *Complete Works,* vol. 6, Psalm 130, (Edinburgh, 1967), page 582.

merely to read the Christian material but the secular material too. We all have limited hours in our day, and only so much time to spare on reading around our field, but it's important to have a firsthand grasp of at least some of what Freud and Jung actually said, and even more some of the developments in brain understanding in more recent years. Read up on the work of Antonio Damasio,[5] or *The Body Keeps the Score* by Bessel van der Kolk.[6] The way people feel is not only solved by cognitive behavior therapy, or talk therapy of one kind or another. Our emotions, 'affections,' and body life, also all impact how stuck we are in various behaviors and thought patterns.

But then, second, I think many congregants are contrastingly woefully ignorant of the real impact of straightforward, Spirit-empowered, prayer-anointed, gospel-driven remedies. Oh yes, the average Christian thinks, if you have a minor problem, then a sermon, or a Bible study, might help. But if you have a really *big* problem, then you'd better go to a counselor, or even a psychiatrist. Now, obviously, I could be charged with being biased here as I am a pastor. But all I can say is that—as I indicated above—while I greatly respect, and work with, professional counselors, and also do not think of myself as a counselor, and therefore limit the number of 'sessions' (to use counselor jargon) I will have with anyone, I have not found that 'counseling' is the panacea for all ills. I remember one person who came to me for help that, after describing their situation, I asked whether any of the psychiatrists they had ever been to had ever pointed out such and such. I was astonished to hear 'no.'

---

5    For instance, Antonio Damasio, *Descartes' Error: Emotion, Reason and the Human Brain*, (Putnam, 1994).

6    Bessel Van Der Kolk, *The Body Keeps the Score: Brain, Mind, and Body in the Healing of Trauma*, (Penguin Books, 2014).

We got to work. This person is in effective Christian ministry now. My tool to help this person? Take a notebook. Spend a day reading through the Bible—as much as you can cover. Write down every promise from God for your situation. And then we'll talk. It was life changing.

Thirdly, my personal approach is to not be governed by a set philosophy. I know people love to have a 'theory' or 'framework' that they can then govern all their details of their methodology under. But when it comes to mental health, I have found the very best way is to listen hard. And I mean really listen. Prayerfully listen. I will gather all the information I can. I will ask as many questions as I know how. I will glean around in the areas of family, and history, and patterns of thought and life. And I will listen. I will listen prayerfully—that is, as I am listening I am also seeking to listen to God. Lord, show me how I can help. Lord, give me insight. I will be praying for areas of that person's life to be softened, or healed, or encouraged, or strengthened. I will be scanning through my mind Biblical passages and texts that apply to what I am hearing. I will listen not only in that particular conversation, but to the many others I have had, to the books I have read, the stories—a good novel is a great tool for psychological insight—the biographies and histories of human experience. And then I will seek to point a way forward. I don't think it's my role to be there for each of the next steps. Someone else can do that.

My family knows that I love etymology—the study of the origin of words. I enjoy words, the way they feel, and sound, and the genetic resonance they carry with them like bags of dynamite, or sugary sweetness, to enfold you or trouble you. Of course that sort of approach to meaning has its dangers: words are not really defined by dictionaries as such; they are defined by the way they are used in sentences, and in context, and dictionaries (good ones) record those usages.

But I am fascinated, as we come to the close of this book—and as perhaps a fitting final word with this appendix related to mental health—to note the surprising etymology of holiness. We saw at the beginning that the Hebrew and Greek words for holiness have resonances related to being 'set apart' and equivalent ideas of being special and different, or other. But the English word for holiness has quite a different etymology.

Arguably, the English words for whole and health come from a similar Germanic root as holy. The etymological root means something like 'undamaged.' Or healed, maybe.[7]

Who would have thought it? The healing you are looking for comes through being holy.[8]

---

7   'holy...A deriv. of the adj. *hailo-*, O.E. *hal*, free from injury, whole, hale... inviolate, inviolable, that must be preserved *whole* or intact..."health, good luck, well-being", or be connected with the sense "good omen, auspice, augury"...' *The Oxford English Dictionary*, Second Edition, J.A. Simpson and E.S.C. Weiner (Oxford, 1989), Vol. VII, Page 53; 'whole... OE. *hal*...The Germanic adj. has the meanings (not all represented in every dialect) of "uninjured, sound, healthy, entire, complete"...' *Ibid.*, Vol. XX, page 291; 'The primary meaning of the word may have been "that must be preserved whole or intact, that cannot be transgressed or violated," which would support its relation to Old English, *hal* whole...' Robert K. Barhart, Editor, *The Barnhart Dictionary of Etymology*, (Wilson, 1988), page 487.

8   Certainly, the connection is not only etymological, though the nuances are too many to deliberate in this context. But, for instance, the list of 'curses' for disobeying God in the famous denouncement of Deuteronomy 28 include this arresting consequence of a lack of holiness: 'The Lord will strike you with madness and blindness and confusion of mind...' (Deut. 28:28). Of course, it is utterly wrong, as well as cruel, to suggest that all human suffering—mental or physical—is always as a direct result of personal sin (see John 9:3; the suffering here was for a salvific purpose).

'Help me to offer a testimony for thyself, and to leave sinners inexcusable in neglecting thy mercy...May thy people be refreshed, melted, convicted, comforted, and help me to use the strongest arguments drawn from Christ's incarnation and sufferings, that men might be made holy.'[1]

1    Arthur Bennet, *The Valley of Vision*, (Edinburgh, 1975), page 191.

# Christian Focus Publications

Our mission statement—STAYING FAITHFUL

In dependence upon God we seek to impact the world through literature faithful to His infallible Word, the Bible. Our aim is to ensure that the Lord Jesus Christ is presented as the only hope to obtain forgiveness of sin, live a useful life and look forward to heaven with Him.

Our Books are published in four imprints:

### CHRISTIAN FOCUS

popular works including biographies, commentaries, basic doctrine and Christian living.

### CHRISTIAN HERITAGE

books representing some of the best material from the rich heritage of the church.

### MENTOR

books written at a level suitable for Bible College and seminary students, pastors, and other serious readers. The imprint includes commentaries, doctrinal studies, examination of current issues and church history.

### CF4•K

children's books for quality Bible teaching and for all age groups: Sunday school curriculum, puzzle and activity books; personal and family devotional titles, biographies and inspirational stories—Because you are never too young to know Jesus!

Christian Focus Publications Ltd,
Geanies House, Fearn, Ross-shire,
IV20 1TW, Scotland, United Kingdom.
www.christianfocus.com